Holocaust

The Incredible Story of One Man's Will to Survive the Holocaust

(A Holocaust Story of Survival and Resilience)

Sheryl Cross

Published By **Elena Holly**

Sheryl Cross

All Rights Reserved

Holocaust: The Incredible Story of One Man's Will to Survive the Holocaust (A Holocaust Story of Survival and Resilience)

ISBN 978-1-77485-605-5

No part of this guidebook shall be reproduced in any form without permission in writing from the publisher except in the case of brief quotations embodied in critical articles or reviews.

Legal & Disclaimer

The information contained in this ebook is not designed to replace or take the place of any form of medicine or professional medical advice. The information in this ebook has been provided for educational & entertainment purposes only.

The information contained in this book has been compiled from sources deemed reliable, and it is accurate to the best of the Author's knowledge; however, the Author cannot guarantee its accuracy and validity and cannot be held liable for any errors or omissions. Changes are periodically made to this book. You must consult your doctor or get professional medical advice before using any of the suggested remedies, techniques, or information in this book.

Upon using the information contained in this book, you agree to hold harmless the Author from and against any damages, costs, and expenses, including any legal fees potentially resulting from the application of any of the information provided by this guide. This disclaimer applies to any damages or injury caused by the use and application, whether directly or indirectly, of any advice or information presented, whether for breach of contract, tort, negligence, personal injury, criminal intent, or under any other cause of action.

You agree to accept all risks of using the information presented inside this book. You need to consult a professional medical practitioner in order to ensure you are both able and healthy enough to participate in this program.

Table of Contents

Chapter 1: Understanding The Holocaust 1

Chapter 2: The Road To Destruction 13

Chapter 3: Camps................................... 29

Chapter 4: The Other Victims................. 43

Chapter 5: Rescuers 55

Chapter 6: The Liberation And After 71

Chapter 7: Never Again 85

Chapter 1: Understanding the Holocaust

Holocaust has been called the greatest catastrophe of modern history. It is described as a horrific nightmare that became reality, a hell in the Earth, the hidden front for World War II, and the War against the Jews. Shoah, an Hebrew word that means "a whiplash of destruction", has been used to describe it.

Holocaust was the deliberate murder of 6,000,000 Jews during World War II. 9 million Jews had lived in Europe prior to the Holocaust. Around twenty European countries are where they settled. Some were playwrights, architects and writers. Others were successful bankers or businesspeople, doctors and lawyers, scientists and engineers. However, most European Jews lived in average households with average incomes. Two-thirds of them were dead by 1945, the end World War II.

German businesspeople, industrialists and scientists contributed to the effort. These people helped the Nazis create a group dedicated to mass killing. It worked with brutal efficiency, and it did so quickly.

Nazi hatred did not just target Jews. 5 to 6 Million Sinti (Gypsies), Communists Jehovah's Witnesses. Gays, labor unionists, Slavic persons, political prisoners and prisoners of war were also among the victims of Nazi hatred.

The Jews suffered enormous losses, and so a new word was used to describe the events: genocide. Genocide can be defined as the systematic murdering of a whole group of people for their race, religion, or nationality.

Who was Adolf Hitler

Adolph Nazirm Hitler has been called a monster and the devil. On January 30, 1933, Hitler was elected chancellor and president of Germany. He led his country to war, destruction,, and death for 12 years.

Hitler, a hypnotizing speaker, used fear and hatred to hold on to power. He understood propaganda's value, and used lies and half truths to persuade people. Hitler held massive rallies and parades in an effort to win support. Nazi party members waved gigantic swastikas in support of the Nazi symbol. They raised the Nazi salute to their right arms, and chanted Heil Hitler, or "Hail Hitler!"

Hitler rose to power during 1930's Great Depression. After being defeated in World War I by the Germans, they had tried without success to get their country back on track. Their government was weakly divided. Many Germans were out of work at the time of World War II. German factories were silent. People in hunger waited in lines for bread with their buckets of currency, which were almost worthless. Hitler provided a convenient scapegoat to the Germans: the Jews mainly. Now, the Germans have someone to blame.

Who Were the Nazis Anyway?

Hitler's party was represented by the Nazis, the National Socialism German Workers' Partie. Nazis wanted Germany to have no Jews. They aspired to make Germany a major world power. The Nazis also wanted the Treaty of Versailles to be abolished.

Germany had signed this agreement in 1919, following the defeat of World War I. Many Germans believed this treaty was theirs. It gave France and Poland land that they claimed to be theirs. It forced Germany onto the responsibility of starting World War I. Germany was subject to huge penalties called reparations. Germany was also required by the treaty to disarm, which meant that its armed forces were smaller and more powerful.

Hitler joined the Nazi party as a member in 1919, when the party was still known under the name of the German Workers' Party. It was an insignificant group at that point. Hitler became the leader of party propaganda. He became a speaker, and then an organizer.

Hitler gathered a group men who were known as Brown Shirts. They were named so because of their uniform color. Hitler designated them his Sturmabteilung, or S.A. (German for "storm troopers") Soon the Brown Shirts broke up Hitler's meetings.

Hitler's party and the subsequent ten years saw many ups & downs. In December 1924 they had less than 1,000,000 votes. The overwhelming majority of people believed that Nazism had little future.

Hitler's vote totaled 13.7million as of 31 July 1932. The Nazi party represented Germany's largest party at the Reichstag. It was the German parliament. Hitler did not win the majority vote, but his opposition remained divided. Hitler was a great politician. He took advantage fo his enemies' weaknesses and played them off each other. Paul von Hindenburg, an elderly president, appointed him chancellor de Germany on January 30, 1934. Hitler was dictator, ruling over other people with absolute power and often using brutal force. The Nazi party, which was the only allowed official party in Germany, was his reign of terror for one year.

Adolf Hitler salutes Hamburgers from his open car as he walks past the crowd.

What was "Final Solution"?

Hitler began to speak and write about getting rid Germany's Jews as early as possible. The Nazis intended to expel all Jews from Germany. Hitler once had the ambition to send the Jews off to Madagascar, off the coast of South Africa. Then began World War II. The Nazis were now in control of countries home to several million Jews. They couldn't transport them to Africa in middle of war.

The Nazis decimated all Jewish men, women, and children by executing them all. Nazi leaders met at Wannsee in Berlin on January 20, 1942. They agreed on the details of the mass killing at the Wannsee Conference. They debated which killing methods to use. Their plan was deemed the "final solution to Jewish problems" by the Nazis.

What was World War II All About?

Hitler promised Germany to be the world's power long before Hitler took power. His plan was for the expansion of Germany's eastern empire. He would first go to the areas in which Germans live. He would then push onwards to Russia, Poland and Russia. Hitler spoke out about his plans in Mein Kampf. It means "my struggle." (Most people thought that his ideas were nonsense. They didn't consider them serious at first.

Hitler began prepping Germany for war in the few years following his election to power. He increased the German army's size. He also built up the German air and navy forces. German industry was also gearing up for the war effort. Germans manufactured ammunition for tanks, submarines and fighter planes as well as bombers and other materials that were needed for fighting war.

The Treaty of Versailles prohibits the creation of armies for the German people. Hitler knew full well that he was not going to honor this treaty. To fool the western powers, Hitler lied promising one thing and then doing it the opposite. He did not wish for Europe to unite in the face of Germany. So he spoke about his peace wishes. He declared Germany's intention to disarm. He was getting Germany ready for another conflict all the while.

England, France France Russia, the United States and Russia were all tired from war. These countries were all victims of the terrible losses suffered in World War I (1914-1918).

Because they desired peace, the western powers failed in their efforts to stop Hitler's rise. Most of them actually signed agreements and other treaties with Germany. They allowed Hitler the chance to rearm Germany. They allowed him to execute the first part in his plan for world rule. They didn't raise any objection or weapons, and Hitler was able to execute these actions.

Germany invaded and occupied Rhineland. It was an area the size Maryland. It is located in southwestern Germany. It is situated between the Rhine River & the border that Germany shares avec France, Belgium, and The Netherlands. Germany was not allowed to occupy this neutral territory according to the Treaty of Versailles. But, the Treaty of Versailles prohibited Germany from occupying this neutral territory. They could have easily defeated Hitler then. But they were divided, afraid of starting another great war.

Austria, Hitler's country of birth, was Hitler's next target. Austria was home of many Germans. It shares its southern border with Germany. It also has a common culture. Hitler worked behind the scenes with Austrian leaders and reached an agreement to make Austria a part Germany. On March 12, 1938 Nazi soldiers marched into the country, taking it over without firing any shots. Many Austrians received Hitler with wild enthusiasm.

This was a terrible time for the Jews of Austria. The Nazis acted quickly to eradicate the rights of Austrian Jews. Eva Edmands (a Jewish woman of eight years, was one of the Nazis' first targets) explained:

Men in uniform walked the streets wearing armbands bearing letters S.A. / S.S. Many people started wearing the Swastika on top of their coat lapels. These were Aryans. Non-Aryans, as I learned, were subjected a variety of indignities including cleaning bathrooms and sidewalks.

These jobs seemed to favor elegantly dressed ladies. We would run to the side streets or cross the street if there was a large group of people. My mother stopped wearing make-up and we wore our old clothes. We wanted our appearance to be as discreet and subtle as possible.

Hitler did not find the Anschluss satisfying. Hitler was now able to see Czechoslovakia from Austria. Hitler pretended that he was concerned about the well-being Germans who lived there. He was only feigning concern to take over Czechoslovakia's war defenses and resources. Hitler once again was able achieve this goal without needing to fight.

France and England were intent on keeping peace. They signed, on September 29, 1938 the Munich Agreement. This agreement gave Germany Czechoslovakia, the Sudetenland. The Sudetenland housed coal and iron mining, chemicals and power plants. It was home to critical parts of Czechoslovakia's defence, telephone, radio, and telegraph systems, as well as important railroad infrastructures. Germany lost everything with the Munich Agreement. It was lost without a fight.

What did France & England get from Munich Agreement? For the moment they could keep the illusions of peace. Hitler had promised that he would not wage war on the Sudetenland in return. He had also made a promise to honor Czechoslovakia's autonomy. The Nazis overthrew the rest Czechoslovakia after a brief time.

Hitler, of all things, had been plotting for world power since the beginning. He had written about these plans in Mein Kampf a decade prior. He had been working on the Nazis' war machine since years. Hitler now held a strong hold with Austria, Czechoslovakia and the Rhineland under Nazi rule. The Western powers realized they couldn't trust Hitler's promises. Their desperate attempts to placate Hitler and preserve peace had dramatically weakened the position.

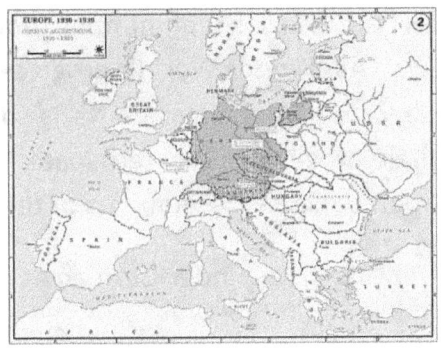

Hitler invaded Poland just one year later than the Munich Agreement on September 1, 1939. This invasion triggered World War II. England, France, Russia and the United States formed what would be known as the Allied forces to combat the Nazis. Germany joined Japan as well as Italy in the Axis coalition. World War II, one of the most bloody wars in history, was a struggle over the future world. It was a battle between dictatorship and freedom.

The Nazis' secret war against Jews was not stopped by fighting a worldwide war. This secret war cost Nazis energy, men, and resources. Railroads required by the German army were often tied up transporting Jews to death camps. Special killing units attached the army were trained for the purpose of hunting down and killing Jews. As World War II progressed and Germany became an enemy, the Nazis continued to wage their lethal war. To exterminate Jews, the Nazis murdered increasing numbers of them.

Europe, showing areas under German aggression, 1936-1939

Chapter 2: The Road to Destruction

Nazis used violence in order to seize power and keep it. Nazis terrorized opposition members for many decades, breaking up gatherings and beating down members of other political parties. After their rise to power, the Nazis took swift action to destroy the opposition. Brown Shirts walked around the streets, attacking and killing people. They entered homes and tore into their opponents, putting them in prisons and concentration camps. Hitler also abolished freedom speech, free press and the rights to assembly in an effort to silence any form or protest.

Hitler's oppressive actions worked. Many Germans did not openly criticize the Nazis when their attacks against Jewish citizens became more deadly. Those who tried to protest were at risk of suffering the same fate suffered by the Jews.

Many Germans were happy to accept any request Hitler made. They longed after the glory days Hitler promised. Many Germans became members of the Nazi party. Many, but perhaps not all, of them participated in the destruction, directly or indirectly, of the Jews.

Europe and Germany did not have a new prejudice towards Jews. Hitler's brutal antisemitism, as well as his policies and ideas, had their roots in decades of violence and hatred for European Jews.

Anti-Semitism at its Roots

The Jews had been living in Europe for more then two thousand-years before Hitler took power. Christians tried to convert the belief systems of a small Jewish minority early on. They believed Christianity was their only true religion. Their goal: to save Jewish people. Their attempts to convert were unsuccessful for most of their efforts. The Jews refused abandoning their faith.

Christians took drastic measures against Jews. They set fire to the Talmud, a collection that includes the Jewish civil, religious, and legal laws. They also prohibited Jews from establishing temples for worship. They even burned Jews to the ground for practicing their religion. Some expelled Jews from the country and destroyed their towns. Others crowded Jews into dirty Ghettos.

To justify such cruel treatment, many people spread lies about the Jews. They accused the Jews of creating plagues and poisoning waters. They accused Jews, accusing them of being thieves and killing Christian babies. They claimed the Jews were friends to the devil. They even accused Jews from killing Jesus. These lies helped those who hated Jews to execute their brutal acts.

From the fourth century through the nineteenth century church laws restricted the rights for Jews. These measures were enforced by the EU states. Jews were not allowed to rent or own property beyond the ghetto. They could not be lawyers, pharmacists and notaries. They were not eligible for academic degrees.

Other laws secluded Jews from Christians. Jewish doctors could only have Christian patients. Jews could not marry Christians. Jews could not talk religion with Christians.

Other laws were passed to make the Jews stand apart from the rest. Jews sometimes had to wear special badges, or carry specific documents. At times, Jews could only have Jewish names such as Sarah or Isaac. They are taken from Old Testament.

Jews had almost all the same rights and privileges as any other citizen in Western Europe by the turn 20th century. Germany's Jewish community consisted of only six hundred thousands, or one percent, out of a total population 60 million. Jews lived and worked all over Germany. However, many Germans and Europeans continue to believe the old lies concerning the Jews. Hitler and many other politicians have been outspoken antisemites.

Hitler hated Jews since his youth. Hitler considered Jews to be foreigners. They were, according to Hitler, polluters, ruining the German race. Hitler's plan for Germany was to exterminate all Jews.

First Anti-Jewish Actions

Hitler's initial official act against Jews was a boycotting of Jewish businesses and shops, which began on April 1, 1933. Nazis erected signs on Jewish shops. Stars of David were painted to the windows and doors of stores. They handed out leaflets asking Germans NOT to shop at Jews. They blocked Jewish shops from entering. To support their boycott, Nazis staged huge rallies. Some Germans refused. The boycott was ended within 24 hours.

Within a week of the boycott the Nazis issued their first anti Jewish law. Many of these new laws reminded me of the old church laws that were against Jews. These laws were issued in 1933 and 1939.

- Forced Jews from jobs within the civil service and industry

- Jews exempted from many occupations

Exclusion of Jewish youth from schools and universities

- Jews had to be issued special identification cards.

- Jews had to have their passports stamped using a red "J".

- Jews were not permitted to ride in the dining car or sleeper cars of trains.

- Jewish and Christian marriages are banned

- Jews cannot hire German women under 40-five years of age;

- For barred Jews, many public baths and parks offer services for them.

These measures, four hundred in total, effectively ended many of Germany's rights and freedoms. These laws also restricted the rights and freedoms of Jews, as well as removing many Jews' ability to make a living. Later, Nazis made Jews wear a yellow Jewish flag in public. These stars were similar to those on the cover.

Book Burnings

The Nazis asked the German people for "purification" of German culture. On the night that May 10, 1933, thousands marched in unison with professors and students. They paraded in thirty cities waving torches. They dumped thousands on books that had been written by Nazis into bonfires.

Dr. Paul Joseph Goebbels (Nazi propaganda minister) was now in charge of publishing all German plays and books. German anthologies didn't include Jewish poets nor writers. Only ghetto editors would publish books from Jewish writers. Non-Jews would not be able to purchase books written by Jews. Jews were also barred from all arts and crafts by the Nazis. They prohibited Jewish composers' works. They banned Jewish musicians and their symphonies.

German galleries did not permit Jewish painters to exhibit.

Even Germany's cultural history had to conform to the Nazi guidelines. Only Nazis approved art was accepted.

The burning of un-German books on the Opernplatz, Berlin by students and members of the SA.

Kristallnacht: Crystal Night

Kristallnacht, also known as "night of the broken glasses" or "crystal nights", is an acronym for "crystalnacht". The Nazis attacked Jewish communities the night before November 9, 1938. They looted and destroyed over 1000 synagogues. They destroyed over 71,000 businesses. They demolished Jewish homes and schools, as well as cemeteries and cemeteries. Anna Bluethe (a Jewish woman) explained what happened to her family in Kaiserslautern when the Nazis terrorized them on Kristallnacht.

The bookcase's glass doors were the first to be retaliated against. All the books were removed from their shelves and thrown out onto the streets. All papers, documents, etc., that father kept in a writing desk, were likely to be dealt with the same fate. They eventually threw the rest of the furniture on top of that safe.

This pogrom, which is an organized display against persecution, was over. Ninety-six Jews died and thirty thousand were arrested. The Jews themselves had the responsibility of cleaning up the mess. Three concentration camps were created by the Nazis for prison space. These were dismal places where inmates were held against will.

Kristallnacht caused Jewish Jews to live in terrible conditions, as Anna Blueth points out.

In the days following, anti-Jewish legislation was passed. They imposed heavy penalty on them, and forced their businesses to close. Each Jewish family had to cover the cost to repair the damage caused to buildings and other properties. Any insurance money which could be claimed to repair the damage had to go to the State.

Thousands of Jews killed themselves. Many Jewish families, including Anna Bluethe's, were able escape. There was no way out for most European Jews.

Ghettos

Hitler's rise in power saw most of Europe's ninemillion Jews living in Eastern Europe. Poland alone was home to 3.3million Jews. That's ten percent off the country's total population. The Nazis overthrew Eastern Europe's Jews, forcing them to flee their homes. The Nazis then moved Jews into the most decrepit parts of the city. Ghettos were filled with tens to thousands of people. These areas had ten to fifteen Jews living in space sufficient for two.

Joseph Soski shared the details of what happened during Nazi occupation of Krakow, Poland by Joseph Soski

They put out new orders and decrets in German and Polish each day. These orders were intended for all people, so they could be used to order everyone: weapons, radios or photo-cameras to be turned over, curfews to be enforced, etc. But these orders and decrees became more strict and exclusive to Jews. Jews in wealthy areas were then ordered to vacate the homes. They were only allowed to bring with them what they could carry, which was usually between 15 and 30 minutes.

The Nazis required that every community elect a council. Judenrat or councils were created to take over the Nazis' work. They coordinated and conducted the relocations of other Jews in the ghettos.

They often used walls, barbedwire or fences to separate large ghettos and the rest of the city. They denied the Jews of the ghettos food, medicine, or fuel. It was difficult to maintain sanitation. Ghettos were infested by lice. The residents were always hungry. Streets were littered in corpses.

William Mishell was a author who wrote a book about his experiences living in the Lithuanian Guetto of Kovno. He explained what happened during cold winter 1941-1942.

For weeks temperatures of minus 40°F were quite common. People searched desperately for a solution. As with many others, our home was well-encircled by a wooden barrier. Each night we would venture out to pick up a plank and steal it inside the house. We were not the only ones to notice such unexpected luck. People began to notice how planks started disappearing everywhere. One morning, people began to notice a sudden rush to the fences. Tens of thousands of people, women and children, arrived at the fences carrying picks, saws and other tools.

Around one percent of Poland's Warsaw Ghetto population (or one out of every one hundred) died each month. But, for the Nazis, Jews were not dying as fast as they should have.

Einsatzgruppen: Mobile Killing Units

The Nazis invaded Soviet Union June 22, 1941. Their invasion was called Barbarossa. The Nazis formed four mobile killing groups, also known by Einsatzgruppen, which was an acronym for "task force" or mobile killing units. These units included approximately three million volunteers. Their goal was to kill Communist officials as well as Jews. The Einsatzgruppen closely watched the Nazi armed troops as they entered the Soviet Union. They surprised many of their victims by moving so fast.

The Einsatzgruppen had the same basic process no matter where they went. They decided to go to a hidden gravesite. With the help from local collaborators, they were able to collect Jews. The

Nazis demanded that all Jewish valuables be turned over to them. They made them remove their clothes. Then, they shot them. Mishell described this as an "action," or the assaults on Jews.

One hundred people were selected at once and told that they were going wash up. After the bath, they were required to take off their clothes. However, when they got to the trenches guards stormed them. They beat and chased them until each of them fell over the other. Although the mothers and children were shrieking, the murderers proceeded calmly with their work.

The Nazis also added gas vans to their Einsatzgruppen arsenals in the early 1942. They forced people into the vans. Then, they hosed carbon monooxide inside. Suffocation was the cause of death for victims. The mobile killing squads had completed their task by 1942. They had murdered approximately 1.4 Million Jews. To find their "final answer", the Nazis turned to another means of killing: The death camps.

German soldiers of the Waffen-SS as well as the Reich Labor Service watch while an Einsatzgruppe member gets ready to shoot a Ukrainian Jew lying on his back in a mass grave full of corpses.

Group portrait showing a Jewish partisan group operating in the Lithuanian woods. Many of its former members were involved in resistance activities at the Kovno gehetto.

For Honor & Revenge: Resist the temptation

At first, Jews tried accommodating the Nazis. They accepted Nazi antiJewish laws. They were determined to make themselves essential to the German war effort. They knew that the Nazis would use brutal, quick measures to destroy any resistance. Their powerful persecutors were therefore not antagonized by the Jews. But the

Nazis' real intentions were clear by 1942. They wanted to kill the Jews.

A few young Jewish men and woman prepared to fight to death in the Ghettos for revenge and honor. They were able to get weapons and other supplies, as well as build hiding places. These resistance groups rarely received support from the rest. The rest feared the same thing.

Only in Warsaw's ghetto did resistance succeed. The Nazis attacked the ghetto with a brutal attack. They also hurled homemade bombs at the soldiers. They detonated mines. Soon, tanks were being brought in and heavy ammunition was also purchased by the Germans. Machine guns were set up on rooftops. But none of these ghetto Jews would give up. The Nazis torched buildings. The ghetto was almost entirely in flames. Three weeks passed before the resistance gave up. The Warsaw ghetto was now a large graveyard, by the time the fighting stopped.

A few young people attempted to escape, rather than joining a ghetto-based armed group. They hoped to join forces with partisans hiding within nearby forests. These partisans destroyed the

Nazis. They destroyed railroad tracks and bridges as well as telephone wires.

Partisans faced hardship and danger every day of their lives. There was very little food and no weapons. They attempted to bomb them many times. Informers informed the Nazis of where they were hiding. Sometimes nonJewish partisans would attack Jewish parties.

To become a partisan was often a death sentence. Some of those brave fighters survived, and they shared their stories with everyone.

During the suppression in Warsaw ghetto, Jews captured by SS/SD troops are forced from their shelter to march to the Umschlagplatz and be deported.

Chapter 3: Camps

Six years after the start of World War II in Europe, the Nazis founded their first concentration station on March 22, 1983. It was situated ten minutes northwest of Munich (Germany), and was known as Dachau. It was constructed by Nazis to hold political prisoners in one location and "concentrate their opponents".

S.A. security guards and S.S. security guards, members in the private Nazi army ran Dachau camp at a cruel efficiency. Prisoners were required to do tedious and often unproductive jobs. Anyone who refused to do so or disobeyed a guard would be shot or hanged. The Nazis wanted all prisoners' bodies, minds and sprits to be destroyed.

Dachau became a model site for larger camps such as Sachsenhausen (established by the Nazis in 1936), Buchenwald (1937), Flossenburg(388), Mauthausen (1938), Mauthausen and Ravensbruck (1939). The Nazis also built smaller camps. Guards were trained in Dachau-style methods to use in their new camps. The Nazis did no attempt to hide the terrible treatment of political prisoners. They wanted all remaining German adversaries to be terrified.

Karl Ibach was a young boy when he signed up for the Social Workers' Young League and protested against Nazism. He was arrested and placed in a concentration facility for three weeks.

They set us useless tasks to complete, like taking stones out the River Wupper freezing water and searching for concealed weapons in sewers. If they wanted further information, they would lock your body in a metal case and turn it upsidedown. Then, before they put it in, they would kick the lid and smoke a cigarette through its vent holes. They beat all those who refused. The punishment for those who ate them and vomited was to eat their vomit.

Prisoners carry large stones from the Wiener Graben quarry to Mauthausen.

The Concentration Camp System

With the beginning of World War II, in 1939 the Nazis started to build more concentration camp. As the German army moved in to Austria and Poland, they established camps in these two countries. These new camps were filled to the brim with political opponents as well as prisoners of war, criminals or Jews. Anyone who was considered a threat by the Nazis, such as ministers or priests, could end-up in a camp.

In the early 1940s, Nazis transformed concentration camps into huge slave labor colonies. Germany urgently needed workers for its war effort. Germany's expanded camp system provided a huge and free labor pool.

Many of the Jewish Ghettos they had constructed were destroyed by the Nazis. They gassed or shot most of its inhabitants. But they saved the young and most healthy for slave labor. Joseph Soski worked as a slave worker and recalls how Nazis picked who would survive and who would die.

An S.S. Nazi men stood on one corner of the street and conducted the selection. Each Jew was asked to take a step forward. People with work papers were asked about their age and trade. The Jew was then told to stop and wait. All other men, women, and children, were instructed to march toward a railroad spur.

Auschwitz had Nazis who tattooed prisoner workers to identify them. They did nothing to mark the victims they chose to gas chamber.

Jewish women who were freed from a Mehlteuer factory showed off their tattoos.

In total, the Nazis built 23 major camps. Many of the larger camps included smaller camps, called subcamps. Dachau, as an example, had168 subcamps. Buchenwald had 133. There were over a thousand subcamps. Many of these subcamps contained factories where inmates could work.

The number registered inmates rose from twenty-three thousand in 1930s to one hundred and sixty thousand in 1942. It reached seven hundred,000 in January 1945. These labor camps had a total of

1.5million prisoners. About half of the prisoners were executed.

Nazis also "rented" prison inmates to German corporations, and took their wages. Slavery took place in factories, mines, logging camp, and rock quarries. Slavery was a huge source of income for many large companies. I.G. Some of them, like I.G. Farben, BMW, Krupps and Krupps remain in business today.

The concentration camps were brutal. Guards treated inmates as worse than slaves. They didn't care whether their prisoners survived or died, particularly the Jewish inmates. In fact, they saw camps as another way of getting rid of Jews. Prisoners worked hard, seven days a semaine, for long periods of time. They were starved and beat, as their testimony attests.

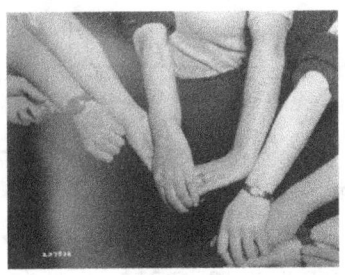

The morning after roll call consisted of one meal. A piece of old bread, a small amount of marmalade, occasionally a piece worm-eating cheese, and a cup of coffee-colored fluid. We began to dig trenches through the forest. My feet were freezing. I was beaten and hit twenty-five different times. My nose was broken with broken ribs.

"Living" in such terrible conditions meant that we slept on the floors, covered in clothes, squeezed into each other like sardines. The conditions of sanitation [were] horrible. The only toilet had a terrible stench. It was full of human waste. We tried to kill these guys, but no luck. There were no washrooms.

Disease was caused by poor sanitation. Inhumane guards tortured and humiliated prisoners to make matters worse. Nazi doctors did cruel and fake experiments on prison prisoners, often with young children. As another prisoner explained:

You would do anything if they asked you to. There was no "yes" or "no", and no "choices." I spent eleven months at the crematorium. I was witness to Dr. Mengele's experiment on children. I knew the children who turned into vegetables. Later, I saw Ilse Kohl with a regulator and a water hose trying to force a hole into a woman's stomach. I saw them cut up... people.

The Killing Camps

Hitler had made his final decision to kill all European Jews in 1941. Hitler's plan could be carried out by using concentration camps to put Jewish inmates to their deaths. This method was called labor extermination. But, it was too slow for Nazis and proved to be a slow method to rid Jews.

They wanted a quick "solution". One answer was the Einsatzgruppen. These mobile killing squads had some shortcomings. The public was too aware of the massacres. Even worse, the gas vans would break down during bad weather. Sometimes squad members suffered headaches while unloading the vans. Civilians also took pictures and occasionally watched. S.S. also took a beating from the bloodshed. Numerous troopers drank heavily and had nervous breakdowns.

So, the Nazis discovered another solution. This one was speedy, neat, secret, and worked for a little while. They opened death camps for Poles. Chelmno became the first of these death camps in late 1941. Belzec was opened in 1942. Sobibor followed shortly after. Majdanek und Treblinka, which were two labor camps, were transformed into death camps that year. The Nazi death camps served one purpose: mass murder of Jews and Gypsies. The Nazis created gas chambers in these camps which killed thousands each day.

To conceal what they were doing, the Nazis built these centers of death in remote areas. The Nazis deceived their victims to keep their secretes and their activities secret. They didn't want prisoners to resist. They knew that resistance would make their job more difficult for S.S. soldiers. The Nazis also told their victims they were going to labor camp. For anyone signing up to be transported from the ghetto towards these "labor camps", they sometimes provided bread and jam. The Nazis encouraged the victims to pack their belongings to continue the lie. Sometimes they even made sure that the victims got tickets before getting on the trains.

In passenger coaches, the Jews of Western Europe often traveled with their families to the centers for execution. However, the Nazis loaded their Polish victims into cargo cars and cattle vehicles without toilets. Vicious guards made screams at the passengers and then shot them with rifles. Victims did not receive water or food, some even for days. Many died due to heat and lack thereof in the closed cars. Anyone trying to flee was shot at by the guards.

The passengers realized quickly that the transports were headed to the murder centers when they arrived.

The horrible smell of burned flesh was all that we could smell. They were shouting orders. "Get undressed! Gather around here. They were shaving people's hair... It was completely unbelievable. We all laughed, wept, and laughed.

Helen Staub shared her story in her memoir about how she learned of Auschwitz from a man.

He simply pointed out the window of a smoking chimney from his mouth and said that all the mothers were there. We didn't really understand what he was talking to and he explained to our confusion that their bodies had been incinerated and they had been gassed.

After liberation, Crematorium oven in Bergen-Belsen

Nazis forced their victims out of their homes. The Nazis made the victims give up any valuables brought along. The Nazis then lied to the victims about the fate of their lives. Guards said that they would wash their hair and get rid of lice. In some camps, Jews were offered soap and assured that nothing would harm them. Their guards advised their victims to inhale deeply. It will strengthen your lungs. They marched their victims to the "showers," however, which were actually not showers. The crowded death rooms were filled with poison gas, not water.

Later, S.S. prisoners pulled out the bodies from inmates. Next, they examined the mouths for golden teeth. The bodies were removed by dentists. Inmates then carried the bodies into the large furnaces that were built in Germany. Inmates went through the ashes after the bodies were burnt to search for any remaining gold teeth.

Finally, the gold was transferred to German bank accounts and credited to Nazi accounts. The "blood currency" could then have been used to fund the German war effort. They also accumulated huge amounts of personal property. Soldiers received the watches and pens that victims had stolen. German aid societies received the clothing. Some of this property never saw distribution. Warehouses that contained hundreds of thousands worth of suits for men and women, as well as shoes, eyeglasses or false teeth, were found after World War II. (Samples can now be viewed at the United States Holocaust Memorial Museum, Washington, D.C.

Within their work camps, some Nazis constructed killing factories. Auschwitz's concentration camp was home to the most modern and deadly of all killing centers. Auschwitz saw mass murder and slave work as one thing. This system worked: Slavery and mass murder could go hand in hand. Other slaves could quickly be used to replace sick workers.

As evidenced by the large number of victims, it was evident that the killing center did a great job.

The Nazis were just about to lose World War II, when the extermination camps close down in late 1943. But the secret battlefront they launched against the Jews was successful beyond all belief.

Jewish children and Jewish women, who have been killed, are shown walking in line towards the gas stations.

THE CHILDREN

The Nazis did everything possible to spare the children. Two million children perished from starvation or cold. Nearly nine out ten Jewish children of Europe who survived the Holocaust were still alive at the end of the second world war.

ANNE FRANC: LOST HOPES, LOST DREAMS

Anne Frank is most likely someone you know. Her diary is one our most beloved books. More than 30,000,000 copies have been sold. The diary is available in 67 languages. Anne Frank wrote it during World War II. Mostly, she was hiding from her family in Amsterdam (the Netherlands). Anne's family fought to avoid being captured and executed by the Nazis.

A few weeks after Anne was thirteen years old, the Franks joined the van Pels clan in the "secret Annex," as they called the hiding place. Anne kept a diary of her two years spent hiding. Anne described what it was like to live in the secret annex. She described her struggle with her mother, sister, and everyday life while hiding. She shared her fear of being discovered and her sadness at all she had lost. She talked about her hopes and dreams, including the dream of one day becoming a famous novelist. Anne was able to maintain her belief that "people really are good at heart."

The Nazis raided Annex Secrecy on August 4, 1944. They sent Anne along with her sister Margo into the Bergen-Belsen concentration site. Both girls died in March 1945, just weeks after British soldiers liberated Bergen-Belsen.

Today Anne Frank's diary reminds everyone who has ever read it, of the dreams, hopes and goodness that were lost in the Holocaust.

Subcarpathian Rus Jews are waiting in a clearing, near a grove. Before being taken to Auschwitz/Birkenau.

Chapter 4: The Other Victims

"Jews kaput. Gypsies, too. And then, the Ukrainians.

The Nazis were obsessed in their obsession with racial purity. "Pure" Germans were at the top end of their racial spectrum. Hitler called them Aryans. He said that the Aryans could be considered a master-race. These blue-eyed, blonde-haired Germans were to conquer the world, he claimed.

Hitler wanted to build an empire of Germans in Eastern Europe. His plan was called lebensraum, or "living room". His plan was to eliminate Eastern Europe from Jews, Slavs or any other "inferiors". Then, the Eastern European farmlands would be available to his master race.

The Nazi racial hierarchy was dominated by dark-skinned Slavs, with dark-haired Eastern European Slavs. Slavic people include Russians. Hitler considered them subhuman, and they weren't any better than animals. Nazis also despised the sick and handicapped, gays, and Gypsies. Hitler's lowest racial ranking was held by the Jews. To the Nazis the Jews were considered less valuable than insects. Hitler had a long-term goal to eradicate all these unwanted groups from German "living area".

Hitler's army was moving into Eastern Europe. Soon, the invaders began to execute his plan. They starved civilians, murdered them, and then abused them. They sent strong, young people from all over Europe to Germany to work in the slave trades. Five million workers from Europe were brought to Germany by the Nazi slave labor program.

Many civilians were forced away from their homes. The Nazis sent them into concentration camps and holding areas. Five hundred thousand Germans invaded Poland to take over areas that had been vacated by civilians.

Political opponents were the Nazis' first victims. This group included Socialists. Communists. Social Democrats. And labor unionists. Resistance fighters were also taken to camps after the start of the war. Anyone who resisted the Nazis may end up in their hands. Thousands of Jehovah's witnesses, priests, or freethinkers were sent to concentration camps.

To identify prisoners held in concentration camps, Nazis used colored triangular cloth triangles. The basic camp colors were the same, although there were many variations in their shapes and colors.

Jews wore a second, often red, triangle to form the Star of David. The yellow triangle was on top.

At the end, at least 6,000,000 Jews had been killed by the Nazis. Hitler's Third Reich killed 13 million nonJews according to some estimates. The Nazis were responsible for the deaths of 19 million civilians as well as prisoner-of-war.

People with Handicaps

Hitler considered people with handicaps to be defective. He didn't want the offspring of these handicapped people to be a threat to his master race. Nazis started sterilizing disabled people in 1933. People who were deaf, blind, or suffering from mental illness, like deafness, blindness, or alcoholism, were prohibited from having kids.

Hitler had already found a faster method to assist Germans with disabilities by 1939. The Reich committee for Scientific Research of Heredity was created. Nazis often used fake science and medicine to justify the use of violence and murder. This committee was used to murder five thousand children who were deformed or developmentalally disabled. Many German doctors voted for the plan. The Nazis called their program mercy murder.

T-4 was another top secret program in this "mercy", killing. Nazis were able to bring together individuals with mental or other emotional problems through the assistance of German doctors. These people were transported to numerous killing centers via buses with blacked windows. Victims were led into a room that looked like it was a shower at each murder center. The fake shower was then filled with poisonous gas. The bodies were then burnt. The ashes of the victims were then sent in urns back to their families. Families received condolence cards informing them that their loved one had died naturally.

Information about the secret killing stations was leaked. Some families received multiple ashes urns. People living near the centers for killing saw smoke from the crematoria where bodies were being burned. Children raced for the buses with the blacked out windows. They yelled: "There is the murder-box again!"

Many Germans, Catholic and Protestant clergy alike, protested. Hitler finally stopped the T-4 project. But the Nazis had already killed somewhere between eighty and one hundred thousand handicapped individuals.

T-4 was an experiment by the Nazis. These concentrations were used by the Nazis to develop mass murder techniques. The fake showers, poison gases chambers, as well as the crematoria, all returned to Nazi death camps later. German doctors continued their role in the mass killings.

Sinti, Roma

Like the Jews before them, the Roma and Sinti were considered outsiders. They were a dark-skinned race whose ancestors are from India. They had their own culture, customs, and history even though they had lived in Europe for hundreds upon centuries.

Like the Jews the Sinti as well as the Roma were subject to prejudice throughout the centuries. The 1500s saw Eastern Europeans make them slaves. In the 1600s Sinti and Roma became like domestic animals. Many countries passed laws to protect them.

The Nazis were not the ones who instigated persecution of Sinti, Roma and other Sinti people. They did however build on existing hatreds towards them like they did long-standing bigotry against Jews. They made Sinti- and Roma-based people the special targets of their abuse.

Nazis used their fake science in order to justify their plans to exterminate the Sinti (Rome) and Sinti (Sinti). German doctors used bogus experiments in order to prove their defects. Robert Ritter from Germany was the director for this so-called study. Ritter ran the Reich Office for Race and Hygiene Population Biology. He sent researchers to measure skulls among Sinti and Roma. His researchers charted eye color. They created wax masks of their faces to examine their features. They even created tests to determine if the Roma or Sinti blood was any different from other humans. These spurious experiments were used by the Nazis to prove that Sinti and Roma people are criminals. They also stated that their research proved the primitive nature of Sinti, and Roma.

In 1938, the Nazis began to collect Sinti or Roma people. They grabbed men, girls, and boys from their workplaces and homes. They sent many Sinti Roma and Sinti to concentration camp and holding areas. Others were just killed by death squads. One Ukrainian told us that fascists treated Gypsies "as if they were games."

Gypsy children in Rivesaltes.

Anton Fojn, an Italian, was taken away from his home in a Nazi raid. The ordeal that followed was described by Fojn:

My father was arrested in an earlier raid of Bruck an der Mur. He found out my uncle and I were taken at the railroad station. He asked for the Germans' permission to transport us in the identical boxcar. Two days later and just outside Dachau, the train halted. We waited, locked in our airless boxcars for approximately three quarters. Then, thirty or forty young S.S. personnel unlocked all the bolts and opened their doors. "Austrians pigheads," the men shouted. Run,... run." They whipped us and killed two men as we ran towards Dachau.

It didn't occur to me that Dachau would be as much heaven as Buchenwald. Buchenwald required everyone to run everything. "Schnell! Schnell!" shouted our guards as we tried to pull trees and dig trenches. Blows fell on our necks, backs, and necks. One of my uncles couldn't keep up with the pace. An S.S.man bludgeoned my uncle to death.

Sinti (Roma and Sinti) were starved, gassed, and abused in concentration camps. They were also used by the Nazis for painful, and horrifying medical experiments. In 1940, Cyklon B was tested on 250 Sinti, Roma, and Roma children. Soon, they began to use the poison in the gas chambers within their extermination camps.

Europe was home for an estimated one-million Sinti, Roma, and Sinti in 1900. These people were murdered by the Nazis in the aftermath of World War II.

Jehovah's Witnesses

Jehovah's witnesses are members in good standing of a Christian faith group. They do no enlist to fight in wars or join the armed force. They consider themselves God's troops. They also believe in spreading Christianity's message. They want to convert people to their religion.

Hitler's Germany contained only approximately twenty-five hundred Jehovah's Witnesses. They were however a firebrand for the Nazis. They refused the German army. They condemned Hitler, saying he was evil. They never said, "Heil Nazir!" They never saluted the Nazi flag. Jehovah's Witnesses remained to distribute books and newspapers that carried their message.

In 1937, Jehovah's Witnesses were targeted by the Nazis. They forbade Jehovah's Witnesses (and all other Christians) from gathering or praying together. They did searches for their banned literature. About one in four Jehovah's Witnesses ended a life in a concentration prison or prison. These prisoners could easily be released. All they had needed to do was sign an affirmation stating that they would not have any contact with their group members. Jehovah's witnesses were often abused and forced to do hard labor in concentration camps. Others were shot. Many people were shot, but few signed Nazi oaths.

Homosexuals

Gay marriage was illegal in pre Nazi Germany. But homosexuals were tolerated. Many gay bars existed and progay writing was published in those two decades before Hitler's Third Reich.

Hitler's rise was accompanied by Nazism. They did not want to stop homosexuals from improving the German race. They raided gay bars. They destroyed books supporting homosexuality. They sent between ten - fifteen thousand homosexuals prisoner.

The "pink-triangles" suffered brutal treatment in the camps. Many homosexuals slaved at the rock quarries. The Nazis also performed their fake research about homosexuals. They claimed they wanted the truth about homosexuality. They gave homosexual inmates male hormones. They finally offered homosexuals freedom if the castrated or prostitution-addicted inmates would consent to their treatment. Six to ninety-nine thousand homosexual prisoners were killed in the camps.

Slavic People

Many Slavic residents lived in Czechoslovakia. Poland. Ukraine. The Nazis thought the Slavs were primitive and inept. Hitler's plan required that one third of Slavic people be sent to Asia by the Germans, one third would be killed, and the remaining third would remain as slaves. Slavs were not executed automatically, however. Czechoslovakia was an example of this, with the Nazis being met with no resistance. However, most Slavs were spared.

Nazis believed certain Slavs were particularly dangerous. In Poland, priests as well professors, doctors, lawyers and writers were tortured, killed, and even executed. In some places, half of the priests were killed and half of the lawyers were also murdered. They also executed nearly half the professors and doctors of Poland. The Nazis thought that Poles would not oppose the Nazis without leaders.

Nazis drove civilians from homes. They placed them on cold train cars without any food, water, or oxygen. Many people were abandoned at railroad stations and on the open field. Others ended the day in Germany where they worked as slave laborers for factories.

People who are left behind could be killed or taken into custody at any time. Polish churches and schools were also closed by the Nazis. Polish children could not attend school past the fourth grade. Polish art, sculptures, and libraries were also demolished by the Nazis. Similar scenes were recreated as Hitler's army moved into Ukraine and European areas of Russia.

The Nazis also mistreated the 5.7 Million Slavs surrendering to the Soviet army. These men were made to work long hours and were forced to eat starvation. Over three billion people were taken prisoner by Nazis. Few British or Americans were Nazi war prisoners, however. A concentration-camp prisoner observed:

I was in Flossenburg two weeks. They shot 25,000 Russian Soldiers. We placed them on wooden logs to burn them.

Poland had lost nearly three million non Jewish civilians before the end, as had the Ukraine. The death toll in Belorussia was one out of every four citizens. There were an estimated 2.3million deaths. Kiev, Ukraine saw half its population disappear.

Chapter 5: Rescuers

Many non Jews turned their backs against their Jewish neighbors. Some refused assistance. Others refused to help or did nothing. Others supported Nazism. They turned Jews over to German authorities. They betrayed Jews hiding in their neighbor's homes. Some took part in the mass murder.

Many people were motivated to help the Nazis by greed and antisemitism. Aiding the Nazis could result in favors. Informers can sometimes be paid for their dirty work. In Poland, people would surrender their Jewish neighbors in exchange for sugar.

Many people didn't do enough to help the Jews and were just scared. Their fear is understandable. Anybody who hides a Jew could end up in a concentration center, hung, shot, or sentenced to death.

Senitsa vershovsky, the mayor in Kremenchug, Ukraine was forced to flee from the Einsatzgruppen. The Nazis shot him. It is not known how many anonymous rescuers died alongside the Jews they tried saving.

Jan Karski, a spy for Polish underground, is remembered:

To help a Jew during wartime was very dangerous. France and Belgium could put you in prison if they catch your... but Eastern Europe, Poland, can be executed instantly! Execution! Sometimes, if the family was involved the whole family shot!

Non-Jews contributed to the liberation of Germany and occupied Europe despite the immense risk. Some people donated money. Others provided temporary hiding spots or assisted Jews in fleeing to safer areas. Some left food in close proximity to Jewish hiding places. Some Jews took refuge in sewers, after the Warsaw genocide. Polish sympathizers sent them supplies.

Many people passed information on to Jewish leaders, underground group leaders, and other officials who could offer assistance. Liliana Fanysa was the secretary for the Bulgarian "Commissariat for the Jewish Problem." Fanitsa was adamant that the man who planned to deport Bulgarian Jews had been informed by her in March 1943. The deportation order was postponed after the government of Bulgaria decided. Bulgaria was one the few European countries in which most of the Jews survived.

Many sympathetic officials issued fake papers during Nazi terror. This documentation could mean the difference of life and death. If the papers are correct, they could enable safe passage from German occupied territories. They could even allow Jews to enter the Christian faith. Between April and May 1944, the Nazis sent four hundred thousand Hungarian Jews into concentration camps. Angelo Roncalli in Hungary was a Catholic official, and later became Pope John XXIII. He was asked if he could help the Jews. Roncalli approved the baptisms in Budapest's refugee air-raid shelters of thousands upon thousands of Jews. Catholic baptismal certificate served as a passport of escape.

Other falsified documents made Jews overnight citizens within neutral countries. Raoul Wallenberg served in the Hungarian diplomatic mission. This Swedish aristocrat provided citizenship papers for thousands. He also bought housing in Stockholm for his "citizens". Sweden was neutral during WWII. Wallenberg's property was considered neutral land by the Nazis despite it being in Hungary. Wallenberg's home was used as a sanctuary. Wallenberg's efforts resulted in the rescue of at least seventy thousands Jews.

Many government officials allowed refugees crossing their closed borders. Aristides de Sousa Mendes is a Portuguese official who lived in southern France. He gave visas out to Jews who wanted to flee to Portugal, in contravention of orders. His home was turned into a sanctuary despite his government's disapproval. They ultimately took away his pension and job. He replied that he could not help but be a Christian.

Many people concealed their hunted neighbor, often for several years or for days. They put them behind walls, in attics or basements, under floors, or even in holes in ground. Of Netherland's one-hundred-forty-thousand Jews, about twenty-five thousand went into hiding. Anne Frank, her entire family, as well as four others, were saved from the clutches of a few trusted friends. The Frank family lived in rooms over Otto Frank's former offices for two years.

Many families couldn't live together, as opposed to the Franks. Many Jews moved between hideouts. Family members could often be cut off from one another. Many parents were forced by circumstances to leave their children with strangers. Jewish children may be taken in as relatives or cousins by Christians. Families in hiding sometimes had to abandon young children or babies, and pray for a kind person to rescue them. A crying baby can put an end to the efforts of a number of Jews to hide.

Why did certain nonJews allow their hunted friends into their homes and others turned their backs while others refused to do the same? When asked, rescuers often mention their religious beliefs. Others tell of their childhood or a remarkable relative who influenced and inspired them. Many claim they did not have to do anything but help others. John Weidner organized a French rescue group.

I witnessed a group made up of Jewish children and mothers who were being deported and had been taken into custody. One woman had her baby in her arms. The baby began to cry out and made a lot loud noises in the railroad station. The

S.S. agent in charge directed the woman to stop the baby from crying, but she refused. In a fitful rage, the officer took baby from that woman's arms and beat it to death. We heard the mother's distressing cries. It was horrendous. And all the time, the S.S. officer stood around laughing.

I was shocked to see such evil things happen to Jews. I believed it was a violation of my life view. I felt that it was my duty to help these people.

Weidner, Fanitsa Wallenberg, Wallenberg, as well as Souza Mendez were all from different walks of life. Some were high ranking government officials. Some were rich aristocrats. Others were businessmen. The majority were normal people who displayed uncommon courage. Following the war, there were many accounts. They are testament to the many stories of bravery that were shared in times of darkness.

Leokadia Jarmirska

Leokadia Jarmirska lived as an individual in a small Polish city near Warsaw. The Nazi secret police Gestapo arrested Jarmirska's husband for carrying an illegal newspaper. Jarmirska managed to make a very modest living in a German warehouse.

She was fired from her job and quit early one day. On her way to home, she noticed a group standing in front of a store she used to shop. As she moved closer, she noticed a small girl who was less than a year old. The little girl cried out, "Mama!"

Jarmirska realized that she had been a Jewish infant. Jarmirska brought her baby home, fed and put her in bed. From that moment on, she treated Bogusia's little girl as her own.

Jarmirska, with some of her neighbors, fled her home in Warsaw when fighting moved toward Warsaw. Bogusia was on her back, and she carried it for miles. They slept in barns and ate nothing for days.

Jarmirska's husband returned to Jarmirska shortly after the war ended. Bogusia managed to find her father through a miracle. Jarmirska was even further traced by Bogusia. Both men had survived concentration centres. Jarmirska had cared about Bogusia's welfare for three years. She had sacrificed everything to ensure the safety of her child. Now, she had to face the prospect of losing her little girl.

They lived together for some time. They couldn't live with each other. Both had suffered too many in the camps. Bogusia's dad finally brought his daughter to Israel. Leokadia Jarmirska never fully recovered after the death of the child that she had saved.

Herman Graebe

Herman Graebe was a German-born construction engineer who worked in a building firm. Graebe went to Poland in 1941 to work on a railroad.

Graebe, a few weeks after he arrived at Sdolbonov witnessed a massacre near Dubno. He witnessed German soldiers forcing men and women to wear undies. He witnessed soldiers move naked prisoners into a pit, and then shoot them. Graebe wasn't a believer in Nazi murder before he was able to witness the massacre. As he watched, Graebe's outrage grew. He thought of his son, then nine-ten year old. Herman Graebe realised that one day his son would ask him "What were you doing during the war?" What would you answer him?

Graebe was able to use his position in order to hire hundreds of Jews at his firm. He issued work papers for these employees. He provided medical treatment, food, and transit visas. He also passed information that could save people's lives.

Herman Graebe saved more than 300 lives.

Oskar Schindler

Oskar Schindler was a German Catholic businessman. During World War II he moved to Poland. He hoped to make fortunes from the war. He was a Nazi party member, and he purchased a Krakow-based factory. The factory was home to some Jews who were used as slave laborers. Schindler moved into large apartments. He lived a life filled with luxury.

Schindler was soon disgusted at Nazi cruelty and greed. Sometimes, he discovered of Nazi plans to terrorize Jews ahead of time. He issued warnings and reprimands to Jewish leaders. He bought extra food for his Jewish employees. His factory soon became a safe refuge. Schindler's factory jobs were less likely for Jews to be murdered or sentencing camps.

Schindler continued to hire more Jews. He declared that unqualified workers were essential to his factory, and he was in danger. However, many of his workers weren't qualified or trained and were either too old or too young. He was determined, however, to save them all.

At one point, his employees were deported from Auschwitz. Schindler was able to step in and pay huge sums of cash to get his workers back. Schindler also received warnings from Jewish leaders as he learned about other deportation plans. Schindler ended his life in prison several times. Every time, Schindler was saved by the people he had made (mostly through bribes).

His workers were liberated following the end war. Schindler was given a gold band to express their gratitude. They also wrote in Hebrew, the words "He saves one life, saves the entire world."

Le Chambon-sur-Lignon

Le Chambon-sur-Lignon (a small Protestant village) is located in south-central France. Many Jewish refugees fled there during the war to find help. Andre Trocme, Protestant pastor, and Magda Trocme became the catalyst for the rescue. Magfda Trocme was gracious enough to let a poor woman into their home. The woman, who was actually a German Jew searching for shelter, approached Magfda Trcme's door. She was told by the wife of the pastor, "Naturally come in, come inside."

The minister and his wife were the ones who encouraged the villager to welcome refugees to their homes and farms. Le Chambon soon had many Jews.

Andre Trocme accepted the offer to go to southern France's concentration camps to care for the children. Although they were not death camps these were places where many people died from starvation. Instead, the pastor had to hide the rescued prisoners within his village. Le Chambon provided shelter for the children of the camps. They received food, shelter, and clothing. They attended school with local children. At times, they were hidden by farmers in the countryside.

Trocme eventually was detained by French police. The village members found out and began sending small gifts of support. They sent him a piece, a candle, as well as a roll and toilet paper in which they wrote encouragement verses.

People praised Le Chambon's courageousry after the war. However, even the villager did not boast about their heroic deeds. Lesley Maber lived in Le Chambon, from 1939-1982. It was only logical.

Juliette Usach and four of her boys are sitting beneath a sign to direct them to Le Chambon-sur-Lignon.

Juliette Usach, a Spanian-born doctor, was born in Spain. She was the director of La Guespy's children's home, which was operated by Secours Suisse aux enfants in Le Chambon-sur-Lignon. In 1990, she was posthumously proclaimed one of the Righteous Among the Nations.

Adelaide Hautval

Even in death camps, prisoners were saved by people who risked everything to save them. Adelaide Hautval was one among these rescuers. She protested against the brutal treatment of Jews in France, and was therefore sent by the Gestapo to Auschwitz. She ended-up in the area where Dr. Mengele's horrific experiments on prisoners took place. She refused her cooperation. Hautval kept a secret and nursed patients during a Typhoid Epidemic.

Her kindness was recognized by the inmates as "The Angel-in-White" and "The Saint." To her fellow patients, she stated, "Here, we are all sentenced to death." Let us be human beings as long we live.

Denmark, Finland Finland Bulgaria Italy

The fates for Jews varied from one country in occupied Europe to the other. The Nazis exterminated Jews from Poland, Hungary and Czechoslovakia. In Poland, 90 percent died. However, Denmark's Jews managed to survive over 95 per cent. The survival rate was higher for Jews from Italy and Bulgaria than it was for Jews in Finland.

There were many reasons why these differences occurred. The attitudes of the citizens in each country was an important factor. Eastern Europe has a long history of brutal anti-Semitism. Denmark and Finland are, in contrast, open to Jews. The Jews lived in Italy for over two thousandyears. An underground, which is a group working in secret to defeat the Nazis, helped each country to pass Nazi plans for the death of the Jews. This information allowed sympathizers to carry out rescue operations in Denmark (Finland), and Bulgaria.

Germany had Italy as its ally in World War II. But, even so, they refused to cooperate with Nazi's "final solutions." They refused the execution of racial laws or the deportation of Italian Jews. Germany occupied Italy in 1943. Many Italians were able to protect the Jews during this roundup. Some hiding Jews and helping them escape. Others issued fake papers. Many Jews found sanctuary in monasteries or convents and churches. Jews were also assisted by the Italian Army.

Many Danes organized resistance against the Nazi occupation that began when it was first started. They began to collect weapons. They set up an illegal printing machine. They also carried out strikes and sabotage as well as riots. In 1943, it was reported that the Germans had plans to capture Danish Jews on Rosh Hashanah. Rosh Hashanah is the Jewish New Year and holy holiday. Georg Ferdinand Duckwitz a German naval officers was the source.

The Danish people reacted quickly. They assisted the Jews in crossing the water to safety, coordinating their efforts. Most Danish citizens helped. They also donated money, food, shelter, boats and money. The rescue effort continued for two more weeks. It didn't end when 7,220 Danish Jews were rescued. The Danes maintained Jewish property and homes and even their pets and plant until the owners returned. Later, the government offered new homes and apartments for those Jews who had been displaced.

Danish fishermen (foreground), ferry a boatload fugitives across a narrow sound towards neutral Sweden.

Yad Vashem

Yad Vashem is an Israeli memorial on a Jerusalem hillside. Yad Vashem stands as a memorial for Holocaust survivors and the people who fought to save them. It has a museum, a Pillar of Heroism (a synagogue), a Hall of Remembrance and Hall of Names as well a Holocaust research centre. Many trees are found on the path leading to Yad Vashem and the knoll that lies behind it. These carobs were planted in honor and memory of non-Jews who gave up their lives to save Jews at the Holocaust. These heroes, known as Hasidei Umot HaOlam in Hebrew are "the Righteous between Nations of the World"

As of January 1, 2014 25271 rescuers had already been recognized by Hasidei Umot Ha -Olam.

Chapter 6: The Liberation and After

The Nazis tried covering up evidence from the death camps while Allied troops were moving towards the occupied territories in 1944. They destroyed gas chambers. They set fire to storage areas containing the inmates' stolen goods. They destroyed records. They planted trees and buried bodies to cover their mass murders. They sent the prisoners to death marches far from their camps, away the troops that could liberate them. Many people died from hunger and sickness during these long marches. Those who couldn't keep up were fired. The Nazis lost their time.

Soviet soldiers were the ones who liberated the death camps. They liberated Majdanek near Lublin (Poland) on July 23, 444. Soviet journalists and photographers reported the grim facts: gas chambers where 250 people at a time had died; a storehouse with eight-hundred-thousand shoes; one thousand people clinging to life.

However, the Soviet report was initially rejected by the vast majority of the rest of the world. The Germans called them propaganda. They claimed the Russians were spreading these stories in order to undermine the Nazis. The Allies at first agreed that the Soviet reports were exaggerated.

But, the Allies quickly realized that the Soviet records were not exaggerated and represented only a small fraction of the terrible reality.

American scouts, Fourth Armored Division, discovered Ohrdruf laborcamp, a subcamp within Buchenwald. It was a small settlement, one of many that were liberated by both the Americans and the British. The soldiers found piles filled with corpses, tortured and killed tools, as well walking skeletons.

General Dwight D. Eisenhower commanded all American troops present to tour Ohrdruf, after having viewed the camp. He stated, "We are told that American soldiers don't know what they are fighting for," "Now, at the least, he knows what he fights against."

The British entered Bergen-Belsen, April 15. They found sixty thousand prisoner barely surviving. They found thousands of unburied bodies on the grounds. A typhus epidemic erupted. Images, films, and news reports about the liberated camp were circulated all over the world. Gradually, all of the horrors perpetrated by Nazis began sinking in and was recognized by the rest of world.

During April, American soldiers liberated Buchenwald, Nordhausen, Ohrdruf, Landsberg, Woebelein, Gunskirchen, Ebensee, Flossenburg, and Dachau. The troops were shocked by the things they saw.

Oh, the smells! Well, there's no way to describe these odors... there was a combat group that had been through the invasion. These men were nauseated, vomiting, throwing up, or just plain seeing it.

--C.W. Doughty - Liberator of Nordhausen

The first thing I saw was an enormous stack of bodies measuring about, oh. 20 feet long and about as high as a man could reach. This looked a lot like cordwood. What I will always remember was the fact people still blinking a little bit deep within the stack.

Jack Hallett - Liberator of Dachau

We were all used to death. Then you see a guy so miserable that you could almost read a newspaper though him.

--Herb Butt: The liberator of Dachau

Mauthausen survivors cheered the Eleventh Armored Division Soldiers of the U.S. Third Army on the first day of their liberation.

American troops entered Mauthausen und Gusen in early May. The war was finally over just a few short days. The next step was to take care of survivors and to bury the dead. The townspeople in many places were forced to help with the burying of bodies and see the camps. They excavated trenches in order to transport the bodies to mass graves. Troops distributed food to survivors and water. Infirmaries are set up nearby by teams of doctors and nurses. Other camps had soldiers transport survivors to hospitals.

People with contagious conditions such as diphtheria or typhus had to be isolated. Some of these people suffered from infection. Others required special diets. Some patients were so weak and thin they had to be given liquids via special tubes.

Many victims died in the first weeks of liberation despite efforts to help. Mauthausen, in particular, saw the death of at least 200 former inmates every day. Dachau was similar with nearly one hundred and forty patients each day dying. Medical rescue efforts began to pay dividends by the end Juni. Mauthausen had a death rate of between five to fifteen per week.

Bergen-Belsen survivors can cook over an open fireplace next to a mound if shoes.

Displaced Persons

Some liberated prisoners managed to find their way back home once they were freed. About thirty million people were left stranded far from their homes at the end of war. Many didn't have anywhere to go. These displaced individuals, or DPs for short, included Sinti, Jews, Sinti, political prisoner, and slave laborers of many countries.

Some DPs resisted the idea of returning to their former homelands. Many Poles worried about returning to Poland after the country fell under Communist control. Many Eastern European Jews had lost everything in the Holocaust: family, housing and careers. They had no place to go. They also feared that new waves anti-Semitism would hit their countries. Their fears were justified because civilians had already attacked, murdered and robbed some Jewish survivors en route home.

Many DPs ended their lives in DP Camps. They were former army barracks, or slave labor camps. While conditions varied widely, many were very poor. Many DP camp were cramped and inhospitable. Some camps kept displaced persons in solitary confinement behind barbed-wire fences. The DPs didn't always have the attention they needed or feared.

President Harry S. Truman had Earl G. Harrison, the state department, report on the conditions of DP camp conditions in August 1945. Harrison's sympathetic reports led to some changes within those camps.

Most DPs became settled over time. Many Jewish survivors have found new homes in Western Europe. South America, Australia, South America, South America, South Africa, and South Africa. Others sought to establish a Jewish homeland and moved to Palestine, which also includes Israel. Israel became a country on May 14, 1948.

Jewish displaced persons lead a memorial to Theodore Herzl (and Chaim Nachman Bialik) in a Rome hospital.

Nuremberg Trials

Much of Europe was devastated by World War II. Hitler's dream about world conquest had killed 35 million people. Nazi efforts to wipe out all Jews in Europe were close to succeeding. Incontestable evidence of mass executions, slave labor, torture and brutality shock humanity. The Nazis deserve to be punished. Hitler died on April 30, 1945, while Soviet, American and British soldiers closed in on Germany.

Two years earlier, the Allies had already decided that Nazi leaders would be punished. In those days, there were many reports of Nazi violence in the occupied territories. The United Nations War Crimes Commission gathered in London, October 26, 1943 for the first time. This commission helped to gather evidence of war crimes, and to identify the perpetrators.

The first war crimes trial began in Nuremberg Germany on October 18, 1945. Because this was the Nazis' "spiritual capital", the Allies chose it.

The Nazis had held huge rallies in Nuremberg. They had cheered Hitler's hatred-filled speeches there. They had also passed laws in Nuremberg which would exterminate the rights and freedoms of German Jews.

The Allies charged 24 Nazi leaders, and six Nazi organizations. The four hour-long process of reading the charges took. They accused the criminals of the following kinds of crimes:

Crimes against Peace

War Crimes. Violations against the customs or war by killing, mistreating deporting and enslaving civilians; and destroying cities, towns and villages for no military purpose.

Crimes against the Humanity: Enslaving, deporting, mistreating, killing, enslaving, mistreating, and murdering civilians for religious. racial. or political reasons.

From October 1, 1946, the trials lasted close to a year. All but two defendants pleaded "not guilty" They argued that the orders they had been given were followed.

The prosecution showed at one stage of the trial a documentary that covered the Nazi concentration camps during liberation. The judges were dissatisfied when the lights switched on again. The defendants sat still.

One defendant committed suicide while the other was tried. An elderly defendant, who was very ill and likely to die, did not appear at trial. Twelve defendants were sentenced. Three to death, three life imprisonment, and four long prison sentences. Three were found not guilty.

Many Nazis have been tried and convicted since the Nuremberg trials. For crimes against humanity there is no statute that limits their punishment. So Nazi criminals can still be tried and convicted, no matter how many years have passed since their crimes were committed.

Survivors

Holocaust victims are still suffering from the consequences of this terror long after the Nuremberg trials. The scars left behind by the trauma of abuse or mistreatment will never heal. Eva Fahidi, 49-year-old sister of a Holocaust victim, stated it this way:

It does not help. It only makes it worse. The best thing is to learn how to cope with such trauma.

Another Jewish victim that lost his home and family is explained:

Surviving the Holocaust is a sign that your heart is broken. It might be temporary, but it won't last forever.

Many survivors moved on to new lives with new partners, new homes, and new career opportunities. Some were able to share their experiences with the rest of the world. Others chose not speak out about their horrendous experiences. Many survivors found that the world was unwilling to listen or care enough about their stories. The Holocaust left many Holocaust survivors with heavy emotional burdens that they were unable to let go of. Vivid nightmares persisted, with dogs barking, German soldiers chasing them and Nazis screaming "Dirty Jews." Some survivors, who were still traumatized from the starvation diet at Camps, woke up in the middle of the night and required food. For others, loud noises such as the ringing of a telephone continued to trigger fear.

Some survivors have written personal memoirs in order to grieve, pay respects, and bear witness. Helen Staub wrote in her introduction for A Holocaust Memoir that she was a survivor of Theresienstadt Auschwitz, Merzdorf, and Merzdorf.

In memory of my grandparents and for my children and grandchildren, I'm sharing my story. You can't always replace things, but people are impossible to replace. The only thing you can replace is your memory of your loved one. These are mine, to share.

Over time, some Holocaust survivors and their descendants have established organizations to preserve the memory. Several groups like the American Gathering of Jewish Holocaust Survivors hold commemorative ceremonies. New York City's fiftieth anniversary marked a large service. Bill Clinton made a speech. He said that we should remember the years of extremist evil as if it were something we had to do.

Generations After in Boston hosts an annual Yom Hashoah ("Day of Remembrance") celebration; sponsors educational awareness programs; and funds a high school essay contest. New York's

Selfhelp began in 1936 and offers support services to survivors.

Even so, survivors and their children often wonder what it would be like for them to celebrate holidays with a larger family. Stella Kolin, Ira Kolin's mom, was the only member her family that survived the Holocaust.

We're now a small family. I did not have any uncles or grandmothers. We lost our family members and all their memories when they died.

Two Celebrated Survivors

Simon Wiesenthal (Elie Wiesel) and Elie Wiesel both survived Nazi death camp. Both men gave their lives to making sure the Holocaust was not forgotten.

Elie Wiesel

Elie Wiesel (1928-191) was fifteen years of age when the Nazis forced his family to leave their home in Sighet. Tzipora, Elie Wiesel's younger sister, and his father, were both killed by Nazis.

Wiesel became an author after the war. Night, his 1958 debut book on the Holocaust is still the most widely read. This memoir tells of his childhood and horrendous losses during World War II. Wiesel is the author of more than sixty books, fiction and nonfiction.

Wiesel was awarded in 1986 the Nobel Peace Prize. It was for his outspoken protests as well as humanitarian efforts. Wiesel soon after married Marion and established the Elie Wiesel Foundation for Humanity. It is dedicated towards fighting injustice and bigotry.

Simon Wiesenthal

Simon Wiesenthal (1908-1905), with his wife Cyla, were taken to a labour camp when the Nazis seized the Ukraine in 1941. The Nazis then began to carry out their "final resolution" in the year that followed. By 1942's end, the Wiesenthals and their extended families were extinct.

Wiesenthal, who worked in the United States Army to collect evidence for war crimes trials, left the army after the war. His efforts allowed Israel to capture Adolpheichmann, who was responsible the "final resolution". Eichmann, convicted of mass killing, was executed.

Wiesenthal assisted in the prosecution of 1100 Nazi criminals during the years following. He also wrote nine books, including The Murderers Among Us & The Sunflower - On the Possibilities & Limits to Forgiveness.

Chapter 7: Never Again

In April 1945 the Nazi death camps was liberated by the Allies. Germany signed an unconditional surrender agreement at Eisenhower's headquarters in Reims France, May 7, 1945. Finally, Europe was at peace. The Nazi terror was defeated.

Many people at that time hoped to put the Holocaust, war and all its aftermath behind them. They wanted their future to be bright. Others believed the world shouldn't forget the horrors and tragedies of the Holocaust. Many people cited George Santayana's words. Santayana was a poet, thinker and poet.

Those who cannot recall the past are condemned not to repeat them.

Many countries have created memorials, memorials or museums around the world to honor Holocaust survivors and warn about bigotry. In 2015, more than 150 Holocaust memorials were found worldwide. Nearly every country in the United States has a permanent spot of remembrance.

In 1995, a German painter named Gunter Demnig began memorializing individual victims. He used small brass plaques to identify victims in concrete blocks. Stolperstein (or "stumblingblock") is an end result of his work. He embeds each finished block into a sidewalk right next to the victim's last residence. Demnig's initiative spread from Berlin and other German cities to other places, and even to other countries. Over 50,000 Stolpersteine had been found by 2015

2005: January 27 was designated International Holocaust Remembrance Day by the United Nations General Assembly. This day commemorates the 1945 liberation of Auschwitz–Birkenau.

The Universal Declaration of Human Rights

In 1948, the United National General Assembly approved the Universal Declaration of Human Rights. This document lists the absolute rights, freedoms, and dignity that are available to everyone, regardless their race, religions, nationalities, gender, or any other status. A number of articles within the Declaration provide protections from discrimination and bigotry.

Article 2 All citizens are entitled to all the rights & freedoms set out in this Declaration. Additionally, no distinction will be made on account of the political and jurisdictional status of the country, territory, or any other limitation of sovereign sovereignty.

Article 7 All are treated equally before the law. All citizens have the right to equal protection from any discrimination that is in violation of this Declaration as well as any incitement.

Hate Crimes

Hate and bigotry have a hard time. Despite the efforts by many organizations that work for peace and tolerance of all races, hate crimes continue rising in many parts of the country. The United States Department of Justice defines hatred crime as "violence of intolerant and bigotry intended for hurting and intimidating someone because of their race and ethnicity, national origins, religion or sexual orientation."

Human Rights First, an International Human-Rights Group based in New York, and Washington, D.C., conducted hate-crime surveys a few year ago. The survey assessed hate-crime cases across 30 countries. Violence against the Roma was at its highest point in history. Racist and antiimmigrant violence as well violence against Roma were both on the rise. Anti-Semitic acts and violence against Muslims had also been on the rise in many countries.

Human Rights First claims that many nations have either adopted or approved criminal laws targeting violent hate crimes. In over 30 countries, hate crimes are treated as violent crimes motivated through prejudice. A number of countries, including the United States (Germany, Norway) and the United Kingdom (UK), are expanding their hate-crime laws or have already expanded them. The Matthew Shepard, Jr., United States Hate Crimes Prevention Act and James Byrd, Jr. Hate Crimes Prevention Act of 2009 supports the investigation, prosecution and conviction of hate crimes.

However, hate crimes still continue to be a problem for many minority groups throughout the United States. The FBI reported on December 8, 2014 that 6,933 hate crime offenses had been reported to its Uniform Crime Reporting (UCR),

Program. The following are examples of incidents which occurred in 2014

- Three people murdered in front of a Jewish community facility (none were Jewish), by a white supremacist residing in Overland Park. KS

- Pistol whipping by a transgender female in Washington, D.C.

- Attempted Assault, Aggravated Harassment and Threatening of a Muslim 15 Year-old Girl riding a New York City Bus;

Anti-Semitic vandalism, Potomac MD

- During a prayer service in Orland Park IL, a bullet was fired through a dome of a Mosque.

- James Meredith, an icon of Black civil right, is seen hanging a noose around his neck.

A Suffolk County police sergeant took cash from Latino motorists during a four-year period.

Matthew Shepard, Jr.

Two horrific murders prompted the United States government to create federal hate crime legislation in 1998. President Barack Obama signed The Matthew Shepard, Jr., into law. Hate Crimes Prevention Act 2009.

Matthew Shepard (1976-1998) was a University of Wyoming student. He had just taken part in a meeting about Gay Awareness Week. Two men took him to a remote place, tied him with a fence, and beat him. A bicyclist found Shepard the day after the attack. Shepard passed away shortly afterward. This brutal killing brought attention to hate crime based on gender orientation. Matthew Shepard's two killers were each sentenced to consecutive life sentences.

James Byrd, Jr., (1949-1998) was an African American father-of-three who was forty-nine. He was walking back home the night before June 7, 1998. A group of men pulled up and offered him a ride. Byrd wasn't aware that the men were white supremacists who had plans to form a racist organisation. They beat Byrd, tied his body to the backs of their truck, then carried his body for three kilometers. The shocking murder shocked the world. Three years later Texas passed Byrd's hate-crimes legislation. Two of the murderers were convicted and sentenced to execution, while the third was handed a life sentence. Ross

Byrd, Byrd's only son, asked Texas to be kind to his father's killer as the first execution was near. "You cannot fight crime with murder," he said to Reuters.

Genocide

The Holocaust is not the only example of genocide that has been committed in the world. The United States Holocaust Memorial Museum's website lists nine instances genocide. That is, violence against one group with the intent of destroying that group. Some groups keep a list of genocide cases that have occurred since World War II. These terrible events were committed in Europe, Asia Africa, Central America (Central America), and the Middle East. The following chart shows some examples.

* Hutus, which is the majority of ethnic groups (85%), have traditionally grown crops. Tutsis, who are the minority, were herders.

** Democratic Republic of Congo. A conflict related the Rwanda genocide

Learning from the Past

One lesson from Holocaust is that taking actions against prejudice can make a big difference. During World War II, thousands of lives were saved through the efforts of rescuers.

Oskar Schindler, the hero of twelve hundred Jewish rescue efforts, is immortalized in the movie Schindler's List. Today, over seven thousand Schindlerjuden - Schindler's Jews - are still around. This one example shows just how significant it was to stand up against hatred and bigotry for so many years.

Le Chambon's rescue demonstrates another important fact about fighting prejudice: united action is possible. Le Chambon's villages worked together to rescue many. Their success was partly due sharing the effort -- and the risk. The Dutch village Niuvelande likewise came together in support of their Jewish neighbours. Every household concealed at least one Jew. Niuvelande villagers found safety in numbers. They also didn't fear informers.

Also, the fates of Europe's Jews were more varied than what was happening in each village. Germany's Jews lost their homes. Many German citizens fell in the same boat as the Nazis. Many

Germans acted in concert, turned in Jews, or committed murder. Fearing for the safety of their loved ones and their own lives, many others turned down the call, ignored or denied the horror. Everybody worried about informers--even within their own families. Nine of ten German Jews succumbed to their injuries. However, nine of ten Danish Jews survived. Danish citizens stood together against Nazi demands. The Nazis did not get revenge. Working together, the Danes were able to protect their Jews, and very few were ever killed.

"Dad.

Herman Graebe pictured the mobile killing unit at work and thought of his son. He wondered what his boy would think of him when he saw them at work. His son asked him "Dad," and he replied, "Dad. What did I do?"

Graebe had no shame in answering his son's questions, as it turned. He could say that he had done his best to help. His son could then tell him that his efforts had saved more Jews than three hundred.

Unfortunately, most Germans were not able to tell their kids that they had helped. Many Germans claimed that their children only learned of the horrors at home after the war. Many Germans feel that they should carry the guilt for the sins done by their grandparents and parents. Sabine Bode, the German writer, stated that "The Nazis -- first generation -- were too ashamed of the crimes they committed so they covered everything up. It was difficult for the second generation of Nazi parents to confront them. It's now up to the grandchildren, to lift the curses of their families."

Don't Wait

The Holocaust is an example of why it is important to speak out against hatred before they become more powerful. Philosophers said that the real evil is indifference. Good people are all that is required for evil to prosper.

T-4, the Nazi program that "mercy killeds" disabled people, was protested by Germany's churches. These protests had an influence: Hitler eventually relented.

German churches didn't protest Hitler's treatment Jews. The rest of world did not also take collective action. In July 1938, the United States called Evian (France) a conference to discuss refugee problems. The conference had only 32 participants and provided little aid to the majority Jewish refugees fleeing Germany. This lack unified action was what the Nazis took as a sign of strength. They saw this as a signal that they could do anything they liked to the Jews, and they interpreted the West's apathy for it.

Soon after Evian Conference the violence against Jews escalated throughout Germany. Kristallnacht, or "night in the broken glass", was the Nazis' giant pogrom against the Jews that began in November 1938.

How do you think?

Are you aware of your attitudes to people who are different? Are you prejudicious? The following questions should be asked before you answer:

Have you ever made negative comments about someone on the basis of race, religion, national origin, gender, gender orientation, gender identity or disability?

Has anyone ever used an insulting word to describe a person on the basis of race, ethnicity and religion?

You've probably ever heard a friend say something negative or use an insulting phrase?

Which way did you respond? What did your response? What did they do?

Have you ever gotten along with a hate criminal?

Have you ever been bullied?

Are you familiar with hate crimes?

Have you ever been bullied by someone?

If yes, what can you do?

It is vital to be aware about your attitudes. Never forget that prejudice could lead to violence.

What are you able to do?

Each person can take a stand for prejudice in small and large ways. You can be part of the solution instead of part of problems. Here are some possible actions:

Never make an insulting or sexist comment about anyone based upon race, religion, ethnicity, nationality, gender, gender identity or disability.

Use insulting terminology to refer to another person who is not of the same race, ethnicity and religion.

Do not listen to a friend making an insulting comment, joke, insulting term or using this type of language?

Report any hate crimes that are committed in your school, neighborhood, or workplace. Hate crimes violate the law.

Reach out to victims who have been victim of bullying or hate crime. Invite your friends along.

Tomi Reichental, a survivor, wrote a memoir titled I Was a Boy, Belsen. It educates students from Ireland about the Holocaust. He describes how his persecution began at his school of Slovakia. He encourages bullying victims to come forward and help others. He spoke to the New York Times about his message.

If you see someone being victimized don't be silent.

Don't let anyone get away with bad treatment.

Modern-Day Protest Against Hate

Today's hate organizations are in another way similar to Nazis. They too respond to group demonstrations. This lesson was painfully learned in Billings Montana.

On a quiet December evening 1993, neo-Nazis threw a cinderblock out of a window at Tammie Schnitzer and Brian Schnitzer. Isaac, five years old at the time, received large pieces broken glass from it. The Schnitzers have a Jewish heritage, so their window was decorated using a menorah. The menorah symbolizes Chanukah.

Isaac was playing in another bedroom with Rachel and his little sister Isaac when his window broke. Brian Schnitzer then put his children into sleeping bags under his big bed.

Margaret MacDonald learned about this incident from the local paper and called her pastor. Margaret had been active in fighting prejudices in Billings. She had been working hard to get people across town to sign a protest against bigotry. She asked her pastor for permission to have Sunday school children draw menorahs that they could place in their windows. Many others followed her lead. Becky Thomas explained: "It's simple to go around saying that you support a great cause, but it was very different... I told hubby, Now we understand how Schnitzers feels.'

Margaret's idea received support and blossomed. The police offered their support. The local newspaper published an image of a menorah to be displayed in families' windows. The picture was also distributed to local businesses. One business posted a billboard stating, "Not our Town! No hate. No violence. Peace on Earth. In support of their Jewish neighbors, approximately six thousand families placed menorahs on their windows.

The hate groups stopped resisting. The hate crimes stopped. Billings continued their united stand against prejudice. Over 200 Christians came together with their Jewish neighbors to celebrate Passover. To promote racial harmony, citizens organized and attended school meetings. They planned holidays that combined the two. Many Billings family members decided to save their menorahs so they could be used for Chanukah. Brian Schnitzer stated, "The Chanukah miracle only happened after people fought freedom." "That happened in ancient history, but it happened in Billings this year."

Courage and determination are essential to taking a stand against hate. The rewards can be tremendously rewarding, as Billings demonstrated. People working together can make an impact.

The Holocaust must never happen again. It can be prevented by remembering the past and standing up to what is right. Peter Gersh (a Holocaust survivor from Poland) explained:

Surviving survivors believe that there is a meaning behind our survival. This gives us the responsibility of telling others what happened. Not only for our children and their friends, but for the whole world. Never to lower the guard. To stand up to the oppressed. To create a world which is fair, peaceful, and respects everyone's dignity. This would be the best possible memorial to all our family members, friends, and brothers who perished in Holocaust.

The Holocaust's origins

Hitler was supported at the time by those who were involved in violence against Jews in Germany. The plan was soon ready to be executed for the destruction and extermination the Jews. Dachau was his first concentration camp. The SS was the camp's administrator. In September 1935, the Congress of the NSDAP was held in Nuremberg. The tzv.Norimberske laws were approved. They are the regulations that define Jews. These laws made Jews exempt from German society's fringe. November 9 saw the execution of a Jew, who was a German diplomat living in France. It set off mass murders and destroyed synagogues across Germany. Joseph Goebbels, Reich Minister of Public Affairs, reported that anti Jewish riots have begun.

Germany tzv.Kristalova Nacht was held from 9 to 10 November. It saw the destruction of a lot of synagogues and the Sudetenland, Czechoslovakia. 20 000 Jews were transferred to concentration camp in Germany. Heinrich Himmler became the SS commander instead of Goebbels, and was given the task to take 20 000 Jews to concentration camps in Germany. Following this night, further measures were taken to punish Jews (e.g. If a Jew becomes friends with Aryan, it is immediately taken to a concentration center. In November 1938, Jews fled schools and trains. The Jews started to seize their property which was allegedly stolen from the Germans. For Jews in unemployment, forced labor was the only option.

The situation has significantly changed after the Second World War and the occupation in Poland. Behind the Wehrmacht forces were advanced Special Sections SS (Einsatzgruppen), who on the spot killed opponents of Nazism and intelligence officers. All Jews were forced by the Star of David to identify themselves. Poland contained approximately 3,000,000 Jews. At first, there was only spontaneous murder that wasn't organized. After concentrating Jews into ghettos where they were kept, they were then transported to concentration camps. Here, they had to work seven-days a week with very limited food supplies. So it is not surprising that many of the prisoners died from stress and fatigue.

Final solution

T-euthanasia 4 was a first program that exterminated the Jews. The SS began to experiment with different gases and developed Zyklon B a pesticide cyanide. Brandenberg became the home of the first ever gas chamber in 1939. The execution was quick. The Jews were driven into the room by between 20 and 30 people, and the room was then safely closed. Although they thought they would be showering, the gas released by showers instead of water poured on them. Similar to what happened in Poland, it also happened there.

It was only then that the Soviet Union attacked that people began to be murdered really big. Four sections SS Eisatzgruppen D, A, B and C were advanced by the advancing armies. This group cleared about 300,000. But the SS is not the only one to be convicted of murder. Regular Wehrmacht units can also be guilty. To save working people from the SS soldiers, they killed Jews utterly inflexible. In Riga, one officer and 21 people were able to kill 10,600 Jews. 1942 saw the second wave in mass killings. It killed around 900,000. They did mass murder. They brought the Jews out to the meadow to make a big pit. It fell shortly after the shooting. He was also present in August 1941 at Himmler's murders and could not keep.

Another method was tried after this incident. There were once many cars that used exhaust gases. Each squad was provided with two cars modified to suit their needs. They started to use the newly constructed extermination camps Sobibor Majdanek. Chelmno. Belzec. Treblinka. In September 1941, they were gassed by Auschwitz's 250 first Zyklon-B Jews. Lodz was the location of the first Chelmno camp. It was here that he began to commit murders on December 8, 1941. Wannsee hosted a meeting between leaders of the SS, and NSDAP in January 1942. Reinhard Heydrich was the Nazi's leader. Here they agreed to a final solution. The Holocaust took precedence over any war effort. About 8,861,800 Jews were located on Nazi-occupied land. Out of this total, the Nazis killed 5,933 903. Auschwitz's crystals killed 60,000 people per hour. Hoss, Auschwitz commandant claimed that 2.5 million people died in Auschwitz and another 500k were starving or dying at the camp. The Jews were murdered in Hungary as well, Romania and parts of Italy, much like they were in Germany.

End of all killing

SS agents were commissioned by the Third Reich to escort a column to concentration camps in order to kill the rear. Many Jews fled Germany to Palestine after the Holocaust, to set up their own Jewish state. They also started podarilo. In the second quarter of 1945, was established the Nuremberg trial. They have been convicted of survivors and were charged with catching Nazis.).

CHRONOLOGY AND HOLOCAUST HISTORIY

1920

February 24, 2020

Munich announced NSDAP's 25bodovy plan.

1923

November 9th, 1923

Adolf Hitler commanded the Nazis to stage a failed coup attempt in Munich.

ADOLF HITLER 1889-1945

Adolf Hitler was an Austrian citizen, born in Braunau. He was a former customs officer. After graduating in vain from secondary school 1907, Hitler applied for admission to Vienna Academy of Fine Arts. His father, who died in 1903, and his mother, 1907, were both killed. Hitler then moved from Vienna to draw the pension. After a while, Hitler lived in poverty and sold small paintings. In 1913, Hitler moved to Munich as a voluntary soldier and enlisted in German Army. He was awarded the rank as a lance-corporal, and was also awarded medals of bravery. After being temporarily blinded by the gas attack in October 1918 she learned about the German surrender. Hitler later claimed to have made that decision at this point to become an politician and fight the Jews.

After returning to Munich with Hitler in 1919 joined one of the many far-right anti-Semitic groups, the German Workers 'Party (Deutsche Arbeiterpartei), which in 1920 was renamed the National Socialist German Workers' Party (Nationalsozialistische Deutsche Arbeiterpartei, NSDAP). The program of 1920 included calls for the party. Restriction to civil rights of Jews. Hitler quickly became the party's chief speaker in 1921. He also held the office of party chairman with unlimited authority. Hitler was sentenced five years for his failed coup attempt in Munich, 1923. The first volume, Mein Kampf (My Struggle), was his political work. It was written in Landsberg during his very brief confinement. Do you think he was a strong racial antisemite and advocated for the German people to have "living space"?

Hitler decided to use the failed coup as a means to gain power for parliamentary democracy. NSDAP, which he founded in 1928, was not able to win 2.8% of votes in the Reichstag election (Reichstag, Germany's parliament), two years later. However, 18.3% had been achieved during the current economic crisis. Hitler ran for the office President of The Reich in 1932. Although he lost, he received 36.8%. NSDAP gained 37.3% of the electoral vote in July 1932. However, its voting share decreased to 33.1% in November.

January 30, 1933 appointed Hitler Reich President Paul von Hindenburg Reich Chancellor. Although only three ministers were included in the NSDAP's government, she was able terrorize and use her political skills to overthrow the remaining remnants German democracy. She also established dictatorship. [See chapter The end of German democracy]. President Hindenburg's death in August 1934 made him the head of the German state and the prime Minister. He was then given the title of "Leader of the Reich Chancellor."

Hitler, though he was convinced and a radical antisemite, opposed the forced persecution of Jews and supported their removal from the corporation. Despite the fact that anti-Jewish legislation was not implemented for political or economic reasons, it is certain that he was the one who promoted her. 1935: Let you quickly develop the Nuremberg Laws and approve them. These laws were to be used as the legal basis for the extermination of Jews from German society. Hitler began to "prophesy" the annihilation and destruction of the Jewish Race in preparation for war of conquest. In a speech to the Reichstag on January 30, 1939 it made the first such prediction. It stated that if European countries gathered their international financial capital into a new conflict, it would "destroy the Jewish race in Europe". Similar prophecies were repeated many times by Hitler in public during his later years.

Adolf Hitler (and Nazi Germany) actually launched an aggressive war. The idea of approaching absolute vitestvi Germany was supported by the quick victory in Poland and the successful invasions into Western Europe. It was expected to lead to an attack against the Soviet Union. Hitler also thought up the plan to eliminate all Jews from Europe.

Although Hitler's order to genocide Jews and other groups is not documented, it is obvious that Hitler knew about it. It is possible that Hitler had just launched an anti-Jewish policy with great influence. Hitler's orders, a program was also launched. Euthanasia refers to the systematic death of German hospital patients. Victory over Hitler was a necessary component of the war, and the struggle for the establishment German dominance in Europe. Do April 29, 1945. Hitler's suicide in Berlin was just a day before.

1930

14 SEPTEMBER, 1930

NSDAP won over 18% of votes in the Reichstag Elections.

1932

July 31, 1932

NSDAP captured more than 37% vote in the Reichstag elections.

6th November 1932

The Nazi Party was able to win 33% of the votes during the Reichstag Elections.

1933

January 30, 1983

Adolf Hitler appointed as Chancellor in Germany

February 27, 1983

Reichstag fire. It was used to issue regulations restricting civil liberties by the Nazis.

20 MARCH 33

Heinrich Himmler announces Dachau as the location of a concentration prison.

DACHAU

One of the oldest Nazi concentration centers. It is located about 15 km north of Munich. Heinrich Himmler announced its establishment March 20, 1933. It was established less than two month after the Nazis had taken power. Two days later they were transported to Dachau by the first prisoners, mostly communists but also social democrats.

In June 1933, he became Theodor Eicke's camp commander. Theodor Eicke introduced a system which systematically terrorized prisoners and led to the greatest humiliation. Eicke constructed an electric fence to protect the camp from intruders. Dachau was also a SS "school of murder". Eicke In 1934, it was designated the inspector of concentration camp camps. A system was developed that can be used also for other camps.

Dachau, they were first imprisoned as political oppositions to the regime. Political prisoners are able occupy the highest ranking positions in the jail, which allows them to be there all the time. This makes it possible to aid other prisoners. Later they were allowed to join other prisoner groups like Gypsies or Jehovah's witnesses. Gradually, Jewish prisoners were added. Kristallnacht had been in Dachau and was later deported along with over 10,000 Jews throughout Germany. After a few weeks they were all released and the deported man promised to leave Germany. After being in concentration camp, many of them decided to leave Germany and opt for emigration.

During the war, they joined Dachau as well as other groups of prisoners escaped from occupied countries. Dachau became a center for mass murder. One example is October 1941. A number of Soviet prisoners were taken to the camp where they were later killed. Since January 1942, there have been a number of so-called prisoner. "Invalids" were taken from Linz to Hartheim castle. There they were gassed. Dachau's large crematorium gas-chamber was also built, but it never became a place for mass murder. Executions were carried through in the camp during liberation.

Himmler issued a directive to transport all Jewish prisoners incarcerated in concentration camps on German German territory. All Dachau Jewish prisoners deported to Auschwitz. In the winter 1942, the SS camp doctors began performing painful medical experiments on prisoners that often ended in death.

In 1942, a network made up of sub-camps of Dachau saw prisoners used as slave labor for German armaments industries. Dachau's sub-camps housed as many as 37,000 prisoners. The largest concentration of auxiliary camps at Landsberg am Lech served as an underground factory. They were mainly Jewish prisoners deported from the east. There were approximately 30,000 inmates at the time of the massacre, which took place between 1944-45.

In the main camp at war's end, there were also dire conditions. Dachau was for prisoners being evacuated from camps destroyed by the Allies. The typhus epidemic affected thousands of prisoners. April 29, 1945 was the date that the camp was liberated by the US Army.

April 1, 1983

Germany-wide boycott of Jewish shops. Lawyers and doctors.

7 APRIL 1933

Adopted a law (Gesetz zur Wiederherstellung Des Berufsbeamtentums) to restore the clerical-state. Under this law, Jews were freed from the civil service.

21 APRIL 1983

A ban on Jewish ritual killing of animals (koserovani).

10 MAY 1933

Public burnings of Jewish books and authors that were critical of the Nazi regime.

AUGUST 25, 1933

Signed. Haavara agreements between the German government (Germany) and Zionist groups facilitating the exodus of Jews to Palestine.

SEPTEMBER 17, 33

Established Reichsvertretung der deutschen Juden (Risky behalf of German Jews). Leo Baeck (a respected liberal Rabbi) was the leader of this group.

22 SEPTEMBER 1983

Germany excludes Jews from the cultural life.

1934

June 30, 1934

Called. Night of the Long Knives – Hitler destroyed the SS SA leadership.

July 25, 1934

Austrian Nazis attempted coup. Engelbert Dollfuss was assassinated.

2nd Aug 1934

Dies German President Paul von Hindenburg. Hitler unified the office of ReichsChancellor/President and gave the title Leader and ReichsChancellor.

1935

January 13, 1934

Saarland was annexed in Germany after a referendum was held.

16 MARCH 1985

Germany introduced universal conscription.

15 SEPTEMBER 1935

Nuremberg Party Congress (NSDAP) issued it. Nuremberg Laws.

The Nuremberg Laws (1935).

In September 1935, he approved the German Reichstag's (Reichstag), two Constitution laws. They were to serve as the foundation for exclusion of Jews in future German society. They were revealed at a special meeting held by the Reichstag in Nuremberg to celebrate the annual congress for the Nazi party.

The Law on Reich Citizenship, the first of these laws stipulated that only Germans and people with "blood relations" can be citizens of the empire. The first law on Reich citizenship saw German Jews losing their political rights. Instead of being Staatsangehorige, they became Staatsangehorige. Meanwhile, Reichsburger were labeled "Reichsburger" (Reich citizens) at the time of its implementation. In 1943, the Reich citizenship law was expanded by 13 implementing regulations. This systematically stripped Jews from all civil rights. Two months later the first of these implementing laws that decide who is a Jew/hybrid was issued on November 14, 1935.

The Second Law on the Protection of German Blood (or German Honor) prohibited Jews from marrying Germans. Jewish households were forbidden to hire German maids under 40 years of age or to erect an German flag.

The Nuremberg Laws announced that they were no longer exempted (awarded to veterans from the First World War, and state officials who held positions before 1914) of earlier anti-Jewish legislations. These new racist legislations not only served a symbolic function by highlighting the need for exclusion of Jews from the society, but also legitimized a wave of anti-Semitic arrests and storms that took place over the last few months.

Hitler declared that these "individual activities" were against the anti-Jewish terror that was growing. It also provided an excuse for the adoption antisemitic legislation. This was essential to justify the Nazi killing spree. Gestapo officials in regional governments and other government officials frequently sought out the official norms as well as a clear statement of policy on Jews. A lackluster policy is also causing rifts in the party and state apparatus. The public also demanded a clear definition for the public's official approach to the Jewish problem.

The debate surrounding the adoption and enforcement of laws was centered on three main points: 1) the deprivation and protection of civil rights of Jews, 2) Rassenschande or profanity race), issues regarding mixed marriages and intercourse between Jews and "Aryans", and 3) a boycotting of Jewish businesses.

Many Nazi-era leaders (e.g. Wilhelm Frick, Reichs Minister of Interior, suggested that the state should get rid German Jews off their citizenship. Hjalmar Schecht, Minister Finance, stated that they had prepared antiJewish directives and measures in order coordinate all antisemitic government policies. Gerhard Wagner of the Imperial Medical Association presented a plan of action for the adoption of the Law on the Protection of German Blood.

Even the Nazis didn't have a reliable scientific tool for detecting "race"; the Nuremberg Laws were not able to determine Jewish-related grandparents. A full Jew was someone who had at least three Jewish grandparents. This complicated categorization was called "Mongrels". "Mongrels". They were considered "half-breeds" or "polozidy", because they did not have two Jewish grandparents.

"Mestizos of First Instance" These men had the same rights that full German citizens, but there were restrictions. They could marry only a half-breed of First Instance. They had to be granted a special exemption for marriage with a German couple or with a person of the "half-breed Second Degree". We pay every person who had one Jewish grandfather for the "halfbreed first degree." He related to them, although there were some limitations in his choice of occupation. However, it was generally true that their integration into German society is the ultimate goal. They were also, for instance. Conscripted into Wehrmacht and the German army. This will require more complicated regulations to determine which children of mixed marriages or marriages among "mestizos", and what the rules are.

These complex procedures required not only Jews to prove their Jewishness, but also significant amounts of non-Jewish people. They were sometimes required to prove their Aryan heritage in order to be eligible for many state professions. The churches that managed the appropriate register were responsible for proving their "Jewish", or "Aryan", origin. Principles of categorization, including of Jews and "mongrels", under the Nuremberg Laws, could then be applied to other countries occupied Germany or its satellites. These principles were first utilized in

Regulation Reichsprotektor relating to Jewish property, June 21, 1939.

NOVEMBER 14, 1985

The first additional regulation was issued. Nuremberg Laws - These include a definition and a description of a Jew.

1936

March 7th, 1936

Entry of the German army to the Rhineland.

6 to 16 Februarie and 1-16 AUGUST 1936

Germany organized the summer and winter Olympic Games.

1937

March 21, 1937

Pope Pius XI. Mit Brennender Sorge (With a Burning Concern) was an encyclical that condemned racism and national socialism.

1938

13 MARCH 38

Occupation Austria by German army - Ie. The Anschluss.

26 APRIL 1937

Germany issued a regulation that required reporting of Jewish property above 5,000 Reichsmarks.

29 MAY 1938

Hungary had the first antisemitic law that limited the Jewish population to 20%.

23 JULY 38

The creation of special certificates was authorized for Jews since 1 January 1939.

July 25, 1938

Regulation that states that Jewish doctors can only treat Jewish patients in Germany.

6 JULY - 15 JULY38

Conference in Evian. 32 state representatives inquire about possible refugee admissions from Nazi Germany.

17 August 1938

All Jewish men and women in Germany are required to have an additional first-name of Israel.

August 20, 1938

In Vienna based Central Office for Jewish Emigration (Zentralstelle fur judische Auswanderung).

September 29, 1938

The Munich Agreement was signed. Power was granted without Czechoslovak representatives.

5 OCTOBER 1936

Passports containing German Jews must bear the J sign (= Jude – Jew)

28 OCTOBER, 1938

Denunciation Of Polish Jews: The Polish border is crossed by approximately 17,000 Jews who live in Germany with Polish citizenship.

TERMINATION Polish Jews Expelled from Germany (1938).

AUTUMN 38

Jews arrived from Eastern Europe in the 19thcentury. They came mainly to Germany from Russia and Poland. The money is used to expel anti-Jewish laws. In 1938 there were approximately 50,000. Many of these were seated for multiple generations. Many were born in Germany, and feel at their home.

After Germany annexed Austria in March 1938, the Polish government began to fear a possible escape of roughly 20,000 Austrian Jews. The Polish government stopped Polish citizens who had lived abroad for over five years from validating their passports. This law, although already in effect on March 31, 1938 after the Munich accord was signed, foresees checking all foreign passports. Only Polish passports obtained abroad were authorized to be brought into Poland after the 31 October 1938. The German citizenship of most of the 50,000 Polish Jews who settled here from day to day has been lost.

After the German-Polish talks fell apart, the German Foreign Ministry sent the matter to Gestapo. They began exporting Polish Jews to Poland on October 27, 1938. The Nazis thought they would also include children and women, and so they deported them in some cases. Many of the detained people were also elderly, some of them dying during the deportations. Others also committed suicide. Jews were taken into custody as a result of violence and threats to their illegal entry to Poland. Around 17,000 people were expelled by Germany. Polish authorities refused acceptance and many of the expelled German citizens have survived for weeks along with their Polish counterparts. They were all exiled to Bytom and Zbaszyn. According to multiple sources, Zbaszyn had six to ten thousand Jews. Zbaszyn developed a large refugee settlement with the assistance of Jewish aid organisations. It restricted individual freedom. Only at the beginning of November 1938, the Polish authorities decided that the camp should be cancelled and that refugees could stay in Poland. Many of them were helped by Jewish organizations and Jewish communities to obtain exit visas that allowed them to leave the country and settle in Poland. After the meeting with Polish authorities allowed the Nazis temporary back of small groups, he was able to return to Germany and his personal affairs. Polish authorities finally allowed the entry of family members expelled Jews from Poland at the end Oct 1938.

Do Zbaszyn was also expelled Grynszpanovych relatives whose son Herschel lived at Paris and decided on the fate of expelled Polish Jews. Ernst von Rath was seriously wounded when a gunshot from his pistol struck him. His death by the Nazis served as a welcome pretext for anti-Jewish pogrom. Kristallnacht.

Polish Jews expelled in Germany by their Polish counterparts shows that Jewish refugees find it increasingly difficult to flee persecution. These refugees were not only from Poland, but also from other countries that had high tides and prevented their borders being closed.

9 - 11 November 1938

Kristallnacht began in Germany. Many Jews were executed or deported from concentration camps or had their synagogues burned or destroyed.

Kristallnacht (1938)

German authorities broke out into a pogrom on Jews in Germany between the 9th and 10th of November 1938. This is known - somewhat euphemistically but misleadingly - as "Kristallnacht", or German "Kristallnacht". Pogrom accelerated and symbolized the Nazi anti Jewish policy during 1938.

Pretext for unleashing violence was the assassination at Paris' German embassy of Legacniho Secretary Ernst von Rath on November 7, 1938. The two shots severely wounded a Jew Herschel Grunspan aged 17 years. His closest relatives died in the German authorities' execution of the expulsion of Polish Jews (from Germany to Poland) in late October. His parents, and his sister, were among the thousands who suffered at the frontier in poor conditions. Neither side wanted to admit them.

Herschel Grunspan had apparently been motivated to take action in an effort to get revenge on their parents. Grunspan was initially arrested by French authorities shortly after the crime. Later, he was transferred to Germany and he suffers from his fate.

Herschel Grunspan image taken shortly before his arrest on November 7, 1938. (Photo: Morris Rosen courtesy USHMM Photograph Achives

Young Jewish man took an unwise and careless action. This was the reason the pogrom broke out. Nazis have used it as a pretext in their escalation against Jews. Nazi propaganda portrayed the assassination, which was part of a Jewish plot against German nation. This was an attempt by Jews to cause animosity between European countries. All German newspapers published over the next days featured hateful antisemitic tirades on their first pages.

Paris was also witness to vom Rath's fight for his life. Vom Rath died that afternoon. A year-end meeting of Nazi "old warriors" was held in Munich the same evening. This was in remembrance of the failed Nazi coup of Munich in 1923. Hitler was seen ascending at approximately 10 o'clock that evening, clearly in agreement. Goebbels refer to the death if von Rath in a flaming antisemitic statement calling for revenge. It was this speech that present functionaries SA (and other Nazi institutions) interpreted as confirming the antiJewish pogrom. In the morning, it was mainly units SA that started anti-Jewish mobs and attacked Jewish buildings.

During the pogrom (which took place in the middle of September, during the 10th, and in some cases even 11 November), the majority of synagogues or prayer houses were burned. They were considered a symbol representing the presence and success the German Jewish minority. Their equipment was destroyed and Jewish shops were taken. According to some reports, 7,500 Jewish shops were demolished. Nearly 100 Jews died in the pogrom. Around 30,000 Jews - most of them wealthier - were sent to Sachsenhausen, Buchenwald, Dachau concentration camps. They were among them when the Empire committed to exile and confiscated their property.

The Nazi leadership incynically claimed the pogrom didn't happen and that Jews were the ones who provoked the anger. Jews were told to clean up the mess and bring the streets back to their original state. Also, they had to take away the damaged fuses. November 12th was the date of a meeting that Hermann Goering chaired. German Jews were also given a fine for their damage claim and had to pay one billion marks. "Kristallnacht", which was also used in order to accelerate the forced Aryanization (or forced

Aryanization) of Jewish property, was also used. The Nazi anti Jewish policy marked a significant and symbolic milestone with the November pogrom of 1938. It represented the transition to complete exclusion and eventual physical destruction of Jews.

12 November 1938

Hermann Goering was the leader of the Nazi leadership. They decided to save German Jews and pay a fine totalling one billion Reichsmarks.

1939

21 JANUARY 1939

On Goring's order was established in Germany Reich Central Office for Jewish Emigration (Reichszentrale fur judische Auswanderung).

30th January 1939

Hitler in front of the Reichstag prophesied that the Jewish population in Europe would be destroyed in the event war.

14-15 February 1939

German army takes control of Czech lands. Declaration of an independent Slovak country. March 16: Declares the Protectorate to Bohemia, Moravia.

5 MAY 1939

Hungary declared a new anti-Jewish law. The law stated that Hungary's Jewish population was to be kept below 6%.

21 JUNE 1939

Released regulation Reich Protector Konstantin von Neurath on Jewish property.

July 28, 1939

Prague, started by the Centre for Jewish Emigration.

September 1, 1939

Nazi Germany invaded Poland. The start the Second World War.

September 21,1939

Adolf Eichmann Einsatzgruppen commander, Reinhard Heydrich. He ordered the establishment, concentration and registration in Poland of Jewish Jews and their property.

Einsatzgruppen

The Nazi mobile killer units known as Einsatzgruppen, also known as "group deployments" or "special purpose entities", were essentially mobile killing units that followed the German army into the Eastern European mines. They advanced Einsatzgruppen together with the German military deep into Soviet territory. They had mined areas at their disposal, and they were primarily Jews, but also other people groups, especially Roma and communists.

1941-1943. A member the Einsatzgruppe was about to shoot a Ukrainian Jew on the margin of a mass-grave. (Photo courtesy of USHMM Photo Archives, Library of Congress)

The Nazi invasion of Poland in 1939 saw a formation of the initial Einsatzgruppen. These units were following the advance of German army troops. They had as their goal the destruction of local intelligence and the priests in Poland. Not mass murder, as they were trained two years later by newly formed units for the invasion.

Heinrich Himmler and Reinhard Hiedrich issued orders for Einsatzgruppen to follow. Himmler or Heydrich met at least three times before Operation Barbarossa in June 1941. These meetings were between commanders of different units who were familiar with their duties. The formation and training of Einsatzgruppen revealed that the planning of German aggression against Russia was closely connected to the instigation for the systematic murdering of European Jews.

Each Einsatzgruppe consisted in 3000 men.

Standartenfuehrer Ohlendorf is seen in the process along with members of Einsatzgruppen, 29th through 31 July 1947. (Photo: Benjamin Ferencz. Credit to USHMM Photo Archives.

Untergruppen, known as Einsatzkommandos / sonderkommandos were subgroups of Einsatzgruppen. The Einsatzgruppen could ask the Wehrmacht for help, but more importantly, to cooperate with local police officers, whether they were from Ukraine, Lithuanian or Latvia. Members of these local police forces used to be paid from the stolen property of the murdered victims. Nazi propaganda was based in the false assertion that Jews were behind much anti-Nazi activity and had assassinated members of German army. Many Nazi intellectuals, lawyers, dignitaries and intellectuals were among the Einsatzgruppen's commanders. Otto Ohlendorf had several university degrees. Ernst Biberstein of the zvelitelu Zielgruppe C was an evangelical pastor and a theologian.

Einsatzgruppen killed their victims usually by shooting. Usually, Jews were instructed to assemble in a given place, claiming that they would be resettlement. After victims were shot in groups were taken to their graves. The bodies were then buried in masse. In the example of the Einsatzgruppen's most brutal mass murder of Jews, they placed posters all over the city informing people that they were required to gather at the Jewish cemetery. People are encouraged to bring with them food and warm clothing as well as documents, money, or valuables. The Nazis, together with the Ukrainian militia, led crowds made up of Jews into Babi Yar just outside the city. There, the victim was forced into stripping and standing in groups for the series. The group fires the squad. Mass graves were filled with the bodies. Babi Yar killed almost 34,000 people within a few days.

1939-1943. Police officers in civil suits and naked ladies before execution. (Photo: Instytut Pamieci Narodowej. courtesy USHMM Photo Archives.

Since December 1941 the Nazis have experimented in the production of slaughter gas using special trucks and combustion engines. This method for Einsatzgruppen was unsuccessful because it was slow. D Ohlendorf (commander of the group) was also not a fan of this method because it "unloads gassed corpses meant that commando members do not have to go through unnecessary mental strain." This method was later used to exterminate Chelmno by the Nazis.

The detailed report, sent to Berlin by Einsatzgruppen's supervisor during their operations, showed that mobile squads had killed approximately one-and-a-half million people, most of whom were Jews. These reports provide the best information available on Einsatzgruppen's activities.

Adolf Eichmann 1906 - 1962

Born the son to a clerk from Solingen in Rhineland. At five years of age, his mother died. He and five of his brothers and sisters moved to Linz (Austria) with his father. Eichmann dropped out of secondary school. His technical school was where he was an apprentice mechanic. He was then able to take over various jobs, and eventually became a Vacuum Oil Company's salesman. In 1932, he convinced Ernst Kaltenbrunner of the Austrian National Socialist Party to join his ranks. Eichmann was released in 1933 from his employment. The Austrian Nazi Party was also banned. Eichmann escaped Germany to join the SS, where he served for a while in Dachau.

He worked in Berlin's SD headquarters since 1934. Eichmann began his career in the Masons section. Later, he was transferred into the newly formed department, which was responsible to another "enemy", namely the Jews. Eichmann, then, became one of the top providers of anti Jewish measures.

Eichmann had the opportunity to show his organization talent after Austria's annexation in 1938. He was then sent to Vienna for the greatest possible emigration. The Austrian Jews fled quickly, triggering a wave antijudiciary terror and humiliation at the hands of the Nazis and other antisemites. Eichmann ordered the Jewish community under his control to comply with Nazi anti–Jewish policies - this led to the emigration and persecution of Jews. Emigration hoped to speed up the process by establishing the Centre for Jewish Emigration (Zentralstelle fur judische Auswanderung), which was founded in August 1938. It allowed for the rapid and efficient emigration of Jewish applicants under constant humiliation. Based on the Viennese template, Goring ordered in Berlin an Imperial Headquarters for Jewish Emigration to be established (Reichszentrale fur judische Auswanderung), and established a similar panel in Prague for Jewish Emigration following the occupation of Czech lands in July 1939.

Eichmann had a significant influence on the establishment of Reich Security Main Office. He was then appointed to lead the resettlement newspaper Gestapo. Since March 1941 carried Eichmann's "Jewish department" (Judenreferat) designation IV B 4. Eichmann played a pivotal role in the expulsions Jews from the Polish territories, which were incorporated within the German Empire. In October 1940, Eichmann was responsible for the deportation on Vichy France territory of 6,500 Jews. Eichmann maintained a network with subordinates in all German occupied territories and the states that he influenced. Eichmann's anti-Jewish Nazi advisors had a strong influence on policy in satellite states such as. Slovak Republic. Bulgaria.

Eichmann's was the office that banned further emigrations of Jews in October 1940. From there, it was organized stream transportations from Europe to concentration camps and extermination centers. Based on the times and places of the transports, deportees' numbers, and their objectives, regulations were established. They allowed Eichmann to cooperate with other state institutions on the deportation and removal of the Jewish population, in particular Reichsbahn. Eichmann played an important part in the Wannsee Conference's preparation. Its primary purpose was to ensure that German ministries and agencies cooperate to achieve the "Final Solution".

Eichmann personally oversaw deportation of Hungarian Jews upon the German invasion of Hungary in March 1944. Eichmann was able to travel to Auschwitz with his fellow colleagues in just a few short months, from May 1944 to early Jul 1944. This included approximately 440 thousand Jews who were coming from Hungarian provincials. After the July 1944 deportations were stopped, Eichmann tried several tactics to deport Budapest Jews. They were unregulated in the past transports. 76,000 Jews, who were not in Auschwitz's gas chambers anymore, were driven to Austria in 1944/45 by the death marchers. From there, they were slave labor in concentration camp camps.

Eichmann hid in hiding after the end to the war. The Vatican helped him escape to Argentina. In 1960, the Israeli secret agency was found and Eichmann transported to Israel. He was then sentenced in 1961 to death and executed on December 22, 1962. Eichmann's role as the "final solution" organizer sparked discussion about Eichmann and how this ordinarily boring clerk became one major Nazi war criminal.

27 SEPTEMBER 1939

Establishment of the Reich Security Main Office (Reichssicherhauptamt - RSHA).

OCTOBER 1939

Nazis to Lublin are trying to launch mass deportations against Jews in Ostrava.

23 NOVEMBER 1939

Regulations on the designation of Jews within the General Government. All Jews over 10 years of ages were allowed to wear the Star of David Star of David Band on their right arm starting 1 December

1940

8 FEBRUARY 1942

Lodz ghetto was established.

Lodz ghetto

Lodz housed 34% (223,000) Jews at the time of the war. It was also an important center for Jewish culture. September 8th, 1939 marked the beginning a terror campaign against the Jewish and Polish residents of the city. In February 1940, the establishment of a Jewish prison in the northern outskirts the former Jewish slums was announced. Jews were forced to leave from other parts, and the area was shut down ghetto on 30 April. 164,000 Lodz Jews needed to squeeze into the four-square-kilometers area. Over a third of this was not stopped. Between 1941-42, an additional 38.500 Jews were deported into the ghetto. These included 20,000 Jews from the Reich and Protectorate, and the remainder from nearby cities.

In November 1941, the government deported 5,000 Roma in Burgenland. They were also held in the ghetto.

Mordechai, the leading figure in the Jewish government sought to maximize productivity, ghetto utilization, and maximum employability of prisoners. Even that might not prevent overpopulation or hunger. Also, it would improve completely inhuman housing conditions in which the prisoners lived lodzsti. Epidemics and a lack of food and fuel as well as poor sanitation caused 43500 people to die of malnutrition, cold, or other illnesses.

From January 1942 onwards, he was deported from the ghetto and transferred to Chelmno.

Here prisoners were murdered in mobile gas chambers. After being killed, 55,000 Jews were deported to Lodz and 5,000 Roma were held there temporarily. Nearly 22,000 prisoners were killed during the second wave in deportations, which took place in September 1942. These included children, elderly, and the sick. The hospital was first to be closed after the deportations. The ghetto grew into a single factory. In September 1942, prisoners were forced to work as part of the German war economy. In 1944, the Germans declared the ghetto closed. The rest of the prisoners were transferred to Auschwitz's extermination camps at Chelmno in 1944.

Lodz had been between October 16th, 1941 and November 3, 1942 when 5000 Czech Jews were expelled. Only one survived in 277th

February 12, 1940

It was the night thousands of Jews were deported from Szczecin to three villages near Lublin.

April 9, 1941

German troops entered Denmark/Norway's territory.

27 APRIL 1942

Himmler gave the order to establish the Auschwitz concentration camp.

AUSCHWITZ

Oswiecim was the largest Nazi concentration and extermination camps. It was built on Himmler's orders in Oswiecim, Poland, on April 27, 1941. The first prisoners, mostly Poles detained as political prisoners, were taken to this place in June 1940. They were then used for slave labor. On March 1941, more than 10,000 prisoners had been registered. Auschwitz camp was known as hardy. Infamous was block 11, (ie. The bunker was where the worst punishments were administered to prisoners. His predecessor was. Black wall, which was used for frequent executions. The inscription "Arbeit macht free", which was placed at the Auschwitz main camp's main gate, was simply a mockery.

Nazi doctors carried out medical experiments on prisoners, making them the symbol for their brutal exploitation. Infamous Josef Mengele. These "doctors", experimented alongside others.

Sterilization for Jewish women and experiments on children, mainly twins.

Himmler ordered that the camp located next to the original tribe built a second larger facility in Sofia. This complex was called Auschwitz II Birkenau. Birkenau's camp was divided up into sections, with barbed wire charging for electricity. According to BIIb, the following were positioned in 1943 - 1944. Terezin family camp. Birkenau had more than 100,000 inmates. It was built at Monowitz camp Auschwitz III. Also called Buna Monovice. Here, the German company I. G. Farben created a factory for synthetic Rubber. A slave labor was used by prisoners to perform the labor. Auschwitz also had 45 other branches camps. These were where prisoners were forced into slavery, mostly for German corporations.

Auschwitz became the location where mass murders of Jews took place. Heinrich Himmler was the commander at Auschwitz. Rudolf Hoss set up a command post at Auschwitz to coordinate the mass killing of Jews. Auschwitz I established the first gas chamber. In this chamber, the Nazis established Auschwitz I's first gas chamber. They used it to test and prove the effects of Zyklon B, which is a commonly used substance for rodent control. Birkenau built four large gas rooms that could murder six thousand people each day. The gas chambers were made to appear like showers. Victims should be convinced that this is a disinfecting measure which must be passed before they are allowed into the camp.

Jewish migrants from Nazi-controlled states began arriving in Auschwitz at the end March 1942. From July 1942 in France, the first Jews were deported to Slovakia. More than 46,000 prisoners were released from Terezin, Auschwitz and the Netherlands between October 1942-October 1944. Some were temporarily interned at the so-called. Terezin family camp. From 1943 to Auschwitz, transports came from Germany and other nations in the Nazi power sphere. Hungarian Jews became the latest victims of Auschwitz's last great wave deportations. These were deported here from May through July 1944.

Himmler's command 29 January 1943 commanded Auschwitz that approximately 20,000 Roma were deported to Auschwitz. They died most likely in the gas chambers.

The transport to Birkenau ramp was held at Birkenau upon arrival. Selection. This is where SS officers select who will be given the job and sent to the gas stations. SS men are often able to make decisions about survival and death, sometimes based on coincidence or mood. The Nazi concentration camps had many auxiliary camps. Vernichtung durch Arbeit - extermination work.

Prisoners fighting against tyranny camp defied different forms of resistance. Resistance organizations helped prisoners hunt for food, medicine, and documented Nazi crimes. They also attempted to retake political prisoners and prepare them for the uprising. 667 prisoners fled Auschwitz. 270 of these were later captured. Walter Rosenberg (Rudolf Vrba), one of the most prominent escapees from Auschwitz was Alfred Wetzler of Slovakia. An uprising took place in Birkenau Sonderkommando on October 7, 1944. This was a group of prisoners who were working in the gas-chambers. The prisoners managed destroy one of the gas rooms and thus undermined the extermination plan. All rebels were executed. A group of rebels, including young women inmates, were also executed.

Himmler's orders soon saw the gas chambers and crematoria being destroyed. It was necessary for the Red Army to hide the traces and machinery of murder before it could advance. Clearing the camp was a priority when Soviet troops arrived in January 1945. 58,000 prisoners were driven on death march - the vast majority of them were murdered along their way. January 27, 1945, Red Army soldiers entered the camp. 7650 people were found here as exhausted, starving prisoners. Also, a series documents about the Nazi crimes could be used to help them destroy the camp. There were nearly eight-ton of human hair found in camp warehouses along with over a half million suits and dresses for women.

According to different estimates Auschwitz was marred with 1.2 to 1.6million lives. Auschwitz is now a symbol representing the Nazi "final answer to the Jewish problem", as well as the symbol for inhumanity or genocide.

After the war Poland and the Federal Republic of Germany had a series of trials for Auschwitz victims. He was sentenced in Poland to death and executed Rudolf Hoess the Auschwitz commandant. Another trial was held in Krakow the following year. It involved 40 defendants. Frankfurt was the first to sentence 22 others Germans for Auschwitz related crimes between 1963 and 1966.

May 10, 1941

The German attack against Western Europe. They occupied Luxembourg, Netherlands and Belgium in just a few days. France surrendered its territory on June 22.

May 25, 1941

Heinrich Himmler presented Hitler with a memorandum in the form of which he proposed to deport Jews to Madagascar.

August 10, 1941

Hodonin u Kunstat opened disciplinary labor camps.

Lety Gypsy camp

Lety's Gypsy camp was once located at the former site for the disciplinary labor camps. Although the camp had 600 prisoners at its maximum, it was soon overcrowded by more than 1100 interns. The camp didn't provide adequate sanitary facilities or other amenities for the many who were there. They were also imprisoned as men, although they were only in the camp from August 1942. In very bad conditions, they have also vegetated women as well as children since August 1942. After an August 1942 onslaught, many prisoners or their families were taken into the camp. Although there are more prisoners than ever before, the camp remains in a very poor state.

The possibility of legal reunification was also considered in the initial month of the camp's existence. The first was released by large family Slehofrova. The result was. The knowledge commander General uniformed Protectorate was responsible for releasing the prisoners. There were reports of possible release on payment of a fee. According to some reports, the Protectorate of 20,000 crowns was able to secure release from the camp.

Run was another option to get out. The escape from the camp was complicated by a fence which was guarded and protected with dogs. It was possible to escape from dislocated work places, where some prisoners even stayed over night. There were approximately 100 escape attempts.

Josef Serynka was one among the escapes that were successful. This prisoner escaped during the fall of 1942. Josef Serynkovi managed a successful escape to the highlands. He joined the guerrilla battle. He worked alongside the resistance group genetic. Luze, the Soviet partisans. Trebon was the place where he was shot.

The Protectorate-gendarmes were recruited to be the camp's supervisory authority. These were prisoners who behaved in a very crude and blunt manner. Josef Janovsky became famous for his heartlessness as the camp commander in 1940. After the outbreaks of typhus in 1943, he was replaced at Hodonin u Kunstat by the current camp commander. This was to prepare for deportation. A number of gendarmes manned the guards.

It was a requirement that prisoners work under the terms of the camp's order. It included work on roads connecting Ostrava with Plzen. The prisoners also helped clear forests and cultivate crops. Prisoners who worked at remote locations were accommodated outside the camp. This gave prisoners greater chances of escape but forced them to leave their families who remained in camp. In these dislocated places, prisoners worked for local entrepreneurs that purchased the labor from the headquarters camp. The money was earned and should be used in order to pay for costs associated with running the camp.

A balanced diet included breakfast, lunch and dinner. Only the necessary portions were served. Temporarily, rations could be temporarily increased by being deported to concentration camps. It was also reported that there had been a case against a food gendarmerie employee who stole the food.

Habitat, food, and sanitary conditions were often unfavorable. Many prisoners became chronically ill. None of the 30 newborns born in the camp survived. The culmination of the 1942-43 outbreaks of typhus epidemic was reached.

Total went into internment at Camp 1,309, where 326 survived. Another quarter of those held prisoner were released, or escaped. Other prisoners were transported to Auschwitz concentration Camp.

Two bulk transports occurred. On December 3rd 1942, the first of these was known as transport. There were 16 men and only 78 women sent to Auschwitz I. As 417 prisoners were taken to Auschwitz IIBirkenau, the latter transports almost led to the liquidation and dissolution of the camp. While the first transport was conducted on the basis on the yield of preventive combating criminality, the second transport was implemented on the Basis of Himmler's Dec 16, 1942 decree, which ordered transport of Roma to Auschwitz.

The remaining 198 prisoners were then moved to Hodonin in the vicinity of Kunstat or to Pardubice. Only a small amount was released.

Gypsy camp in Hodonin near Kunstat

Gypsy camp, Hodoninu Kunstat, was used for forced concentrations of Moravian Roma. They were there at the start of August 1942. From then, the camp was full of Roma family that exceeded the 800-capacity camp. Conditions in the camp were identical to that of Lety, with similar accommodation, sanitation and catering.

Even though there were no guards protectorate gendarmes, the camp still had supervisory staff. Stefan Blahynka, the camp's leader, is temporarily in winter 1943. He visited Lety camp to combat the effects of typhus. After accomplishing this task, Blahynka returned to Hodonin as commander of camp until its liquidation.

Tabor had more than 1,300 residents. Thus, the camp 194 was a victim to diseases (especially the typhus epidemic), and people who lived in poor conditions.

Two bulk transports were dispatched by the Hodonin Camp to deliver bulk cargo. The first transport (ie. 46 men and 29 females) was dispatched from the Hodonin camp. Asocial) was dispatched by the Auschwitz I preventive crime combating organization on December 7, 1942. On the 21st of August 1943, the second mass-transport took place. The transport was transferred to Auschwitz II Birkenau and taken away by 749 prisoners.

After the departure from the second transport, the camp was left with only 62 prisoners. Olesnice was home to one non-Roma family that adopted eight-year old prisoner. This helped her avoid further suffering.

26 SEPTEMBER 1941

Jews.

October 3, 1941

Vichy government makes announcement of the statute des Juifs (Jewish Statute).

October 5, 1941

Romania has a law regarding the confiscation if Jewish property.

October 7, 1941

Bulgaria has a law protecting the nation that limits the rights of Jews.

22-25 October 1940

Baden-Wittemberg, the Palatinate and the Palatinate sent Jews to France, where they were held in Gurs.

1941

JANUARY 10, 41

All Jews in the Netherlands must be registered

March 1, 1941

Heinrich Himmler had an order to build a camp for Birkenau in Auschwitz II.).

AUSCHWITZ II

Oswiecim was also known as Auschwitz (in German), and was established in 1944 by Himmler. It was located near Oswiecim in Poland. In June 1940, the first prisoners were taken from this location. These prisoners were mostly Poles in detention of political prisoners. On March 1941, more than 10,000 prisoners had been registered. Auschwitz camp was known as hardy. Infamous was block 11, (ie. The bunker was where prison inmates were held and punished in the cruelest ways. Before him, he was called. At frequent executions, there was a black wall. The inscription "Arbeit macht free", which was placed at the Auschwitz main camp's main gate, was simply a mockery.

Nazi doctors carried out medical experiments on prisoners, making them the symbol for their brutal exploitation. Infamous Josef Mengele.

These "doctors", however, also experimented on others. Sterilization and experimentation on Jewish women and children, especially twins.

Himmler ordered the building of the second larger complex in Sofia (now Auschwitz II - Birkenau) by the camp next to the original tribe in March 1941. Birkenau was divided in a number of sections, with barbed wire charging for electricity. In 1944 and 1943, BIIb positioned them accordingly. Terezin family camp. Birkenau had more than 100,000 inmates. It was built at Monowitz camp Auschwitz III. Also called Buna Monovice. Here, the German company I. G. Farben created a factory for the manufacture of synthetic rubber. A slave labor was used by prisoners to perform the labor. Auschwitz also belonged in 45 other branches camps, where prisoners were forced to do slave labor, mostly for German corporations.

Auschwitz became the location where the mass murders of Jews took place. Heinrich Himmler, Auschwitz commander, died in July 1941. Rudolf Hoss was commissioned to build an Auschwitz command facility for the mass murder of Jews. Auschwitz I established the first gas chamber. In September 1941, they used this chamber to test and prove the murderous effects Zyklon B. This substance is often used for rodent management. Birkenau built four large gas chambers later that day, capable of murdering six thousand people per hour. The gas chambers were made to appear like showers. Victims should be convinced that this is a disinfecting measure which must be passed before being sent to the camp.

Jewish migrants from Nazi-controlled states began arriving in Auschwitz at the end March 1942. From July 1942 in France, the first Jews were deported to Slovakia. From October 1942 to Oktober 1944, more than 46,000 prisoners were transferred from Terezin and Auschwitz. Some were temporarily interned at the so-called. Terezin family camp. From 1943 to Auschwitz, transports came from Germany and other Nazi-ruled countries. Hungarian Jews became the latest victims of Auschwitz's last great wave deportations. These were deported here between May 1944 and July 1944.

Himmler's order dated 29 January 1943, saw the deportation to Auschwitz of roughly 20,000 Roma. Most of these Roma perished in the gas chambers.

The transport to Birkenau ramp was stopped immediately upon arrival. Selection. This is where SS officers select who will take over the job and will be sent to the gas stations. SS men are often able to make decisions about survival and death, sometimes based on coincidence or mood. The goal of Nazi concentration camps was to send the prisoners who were selected for slave labor to one of the many auxiliary camps at Auschwitz. Vernichtung durch Arbeit - extermination work.

Many forms of resistance were defeated by prisoners who lived under the tyranny of their captors. Resistance organizations assisted prisoners in finding food and medicine. 667 prisoners fled Auschwitz. 270 of these were later captured. Walter Rosenberg (Rudolf Vrba), a pair of Slovak Jews, and Alfred Wetzler (Rudolf Vrba), escaped from Auschwitz. An uprising took place in Birkenau

Sonderkommando on October 7, 1944. This was a group of prisoners who were working in the gas-chambers. The prisoners managed destroy one of the gas rooms and thus undermined the extermination plan. All rebels were killed. A group of rebel youths were also executed.

Himmler ordered the destruction soon thereafter of the gas chambers as well as the crematoria. It was necessary for the Red Army to conceal evidence of murder machinery prior to their advance. Clearing the camp was a priority when Soviet troops arrived in January 1945. 58,000 prisoners were driven to death marching - the greater majority of them were murdered along their way. January 27, 1945 was the date that the Red Army entered this camp. 7650 people were found here as exhausted and starving, and there was a lot of documentation about the Nazis' crimes. There were nearly eight-ton of human hair found in camp warehouses along with over a half million suits and dresses for women.

Photographs showing children taken from Auschwitz after liberation. (Photo: Belarusian

State Archive of Documentary Film and Photography. Photo courtesy of USHMM.

According to several estimates, Auschwitz was plagued by an estimated 1.2-1.6 million people. Auschwitz is now a symbol representing the Nazi "final answer to the Jewish problem", as well as the symbol for inhumanity or genocide.

After the war Poland and the Federal Republic of Germany had a series of trials for Auschwitz victims. In Poland in 1947, he was sentenced and executed Rudolf Hoess (Auschwitz commandant). In Krakow was also held another trial for 40 perpetrators. Frankfurt sentenced 22 other Germans to Auschwitz-related crimes between 1963 and 1966.

April 6, 1941

German aggression towards Yugoslavia/Greece

2nd Juni 1941

Vichy government issued de Juifs II (Jewish Statute).

6 JUNE 1941

In preparation of the German invasion in the Soviet Union, this was done. Kommissarbefehl (commissar command) ordering the killing of Soviet army Political Commissioners.

June 22, 1941

The Soviet Union attacked in an attack on the German army (ie. Operation Barbarosa). Operation Barbarosa began with the murder of Jews on the occupied territory through the so called Einsatzgruppen.

Einsatzgruppen

The Nazi mobile killing units were called Einsatzgruppen (literally group deployments', essentially special use entities), and consisted mainly in members of the Waffen SS/Gestapo and police forces. These units followed the German army to the eastern European mined areas. They advanced Einsatzgruppen together with the German military deep into Soviet territory. They had mined areas at their disposal, and they were mainly Jewish, but also other people groups, especially Roma and communists.

The Nazi invasion of Poland in 1939 saw a formation of the initial Einsatzgruppen. These units were following the advance of German army troops. They had as their goal the destruction of local intelligence and the priests in Poland. Not mass murder, as they were not able to do so two years later.

Heinrich Himmler and Reinhard Hiedrich issued orders for Einsatzgruppen to follow. Himmler or Heydrich met at least three times before Operation Barbarossa in June 1941. These meetings were between commanders of different units who were familiar with their duties as well as plans for future operations. It was evident that the formation and training of Einsatzgruppen was directly connected to the planning of German aggression towards the Soviet Union.

Each Einsatzgruppe consisted 3000 men.

Untergruppen were called Einsatzkommandos or Sonderkommandos. If needed, Einsatzgruppen sought the assistance and cooperation of the Wehrmacht. Nazi propaganda was based upon false claims that

Jews were involved in much of anti-Nazi activity and assassinations of German soldiers. Many Nazi intellectuals and lawyers were among the Einsatzgruppen commanders. Otto Ohlendorf had several university degrees. Ernst Biberstein of the zvelitelu Zielgruppe C was also an evangelical theologian.

Einsatzgruppen killed their victims usually by shooting. Usually, Jews were instructed to meet at a place designated for resettlement. After several victims were killed, the corpses were placed in large quantities in the pits. In the case o the Einsatzgruppen murder of Jews in Babi Yar close to Kiev, posters posted by the Ukrainian militia announcing a requirement that people gather at the Jewish cemetery for the purpose. People are encouraged to bring food, warm clothing and documents as well as money and valuables. The Nazis, together with the Ukrainian militia, led crowds made up of Jews into Babi Yar just outside the city. The victim was required to strip off and stand in groups as a result of the series. On cue shot from the group, firing squad. The corpses were placed in mass graves. Babi Yar killed almost 34,000 people within a few short days.

1939-1943. Members of the police wearing civil suits and naked ladies before execution. (Photo: Instytut Pamieci Narodowej. courtesy USHMM Photo Archives.

The Nazis tested the production of gaseous from special trucks using combustion engines. This method for Einsatzgruppen was unsuccessful because it was slow. D Ohlendorf (commander of the group) was also not a fan of this method because it "unloads gassed corpses meant that commando members do not have to go through unnecessary mental strain." This method was later used to exterminate Chelmno by the Nazis.

The detailed report that Einsatzgruppen received from their operations supervisor in Berlin shows that approximately one-and-a-half million people were murdered by these mobile teams, which includes the majority of Jews. These reports provide the best information available on Einsatzgruppen's activities.

31 JULY 2001

Reinhard Heydrich gets instructions from Hermann Goering about the practical implementation for the final solution to this Jewish question.

Lodz ghetto

Lodz housed 34% (2233,000), of the Jews, making it a vital center of Jewish culture. September 8, 1939, saw the arrival German troops. It was this time that terror began against the Jewish population and the Polish population. In February 1940 the establishment a Jewish prison was announced. It was located in the northern outskirts, near the former Jewish slums. Jews fled to other areas of the capital and were expelled. On 30 April the ghetto area was closed. 164,000 Lodz Jews needed to squeeze into the four-kilometer-wide area. Over a third of this was not stopped. Between 1941 and 1942, an additional 38.500 Jews were sent to the ghetto, including 20,000 Jews who came from the Reich or the Protectorate, and the rest of the Jews from nearby cities.

In November 1941, the government deported 5,000 Roma in Burgenland. They were also held in the ghetto.

Mordechai, the leading figure in the Jewish government sought to increase productivity, employability and dedication of prisoners. Even that might not prevent overpopulation or hunger. Also, it would improve completely inhuman housing conditions in which the prisoners lived lodzsti. Poor sanitary conditions and an epidemic caused 43 500 people to die from cold, malnutrition and other causes.

From January 1942 onwards, he was deported from the ghetto and transferred to Chelmno. Here prisoners were murdered in mobile gas chambers. After being killed, 55,000 Jews were deported to Lodz and 5,000 Roma were held there temporarily. In September 1942, nearly 20,000 prisoners were executed in the second wave. These included children, the elderly, and the sick. The hospital was first to be closed after the deportations. Since September 1942, the Ghetto has been transformed into one huge factory. The prisoners were then made to work in the German war-economy. The Germans decided to close down the ghetto early 1944. In the summer 1944, all remaining prisoners were transferred to Auschwitz or Chelmno.

Lodz had been between October 16th to November 3rd 1941 when 5000 Czech Jews were deported. Only one survived in 277th

September 9, 1941

Jewish edition of the Code of the Slovak Republic.

September 19, 1941

The Protectorate and Empire introduced mandatory labeling for Jews within six years.

27 SEPTEMBER 1941

Reinhard Heydrich assumed the position of Reich Protector.

29 to 30 September 1941

The massacre in Kiev's Babiyar of more than 35,000 Jews. This was just one of hundreds upon hundreds of mass murders committed by the Einsatzgruppen with the support of the Wehrmacht or local collaborators.

10th of October 1941

Reinhard Heydrich consulted with his colleagues. It was at this meeting that it was decided on deportation of Czech Jews into Lodz Minsk and Terezin. The area was designed to be a suitable location for Concentrating the majority Protectorate Jews. At the October 17 meeting, Terezin was finally selected.

16 OCTOBER, 1941

The Lodz ghetto received the first transport from Protectorate. Five transports to Lodz were required to expel 5,002 Jews.

23 OCTOBER 41

The German Empire has an exclusion policy that prohibits Jews being forced from their homes. This also applies to the protectorate.

24 NOVEMBER, 1941

The arrival of the first transport (known as. Commando construction to Theresienstadt.

Terezin ghetto

1941 - 1945

Terezin, a fortress protecting the northern Bohemian borders, was built between 1780 and 17.90. He was made a town in 1782 and was connected to the military garrison. Terezin's Small Fort fortress, Terezin was part of a system of fortification, well-known during the Habsburg monarchy, as a penitentiary, prison, and penitentiary, for military and political inmates.

The second world War years were the worst time in the history the city has ever known. German occupiers were initially established in the Small Fortress Prague Gestapo Prison police prison in June 1940 and, after November 24, 1941, in the ghetto. The former Protectorate Bohemia was home to Jews. Later, they were open to Jews from Germany, Austria or Moravia.

November 25, 1941

Released on 11th regulation implementing Nuremberg Laws. Stipulating that Jews who have been living in Germany for more than a year lose their German citizenship and all their property is forfeited to the Empire.

1942

January 16, 1942

Beginning of deportations starting from Lodz - Chelmno which lasted until September 1,942nd

January 20, 1942

Wannsee Conference will coordinate final solution.

Wannsee Conference (1942).

A meeting of the coordination of the implementation of the "Final Solution to the Jewish Question" took place in Wannsee on the outskirts of Berlin. It was held on 20 January 1942. Reinhard Heydrich was the convener. The meeting was attended by most senior officials from the major departments, agencies and whose cooperation was a prerequisite to the "final Solution" - genocide of European Jews. Adolf Eichmann, an "expert" in Jewish issues, is the leader of companies. Now, the record is an extraordinary document that offers insight into how the organizers of the "final resolution" thought.

Heydrich's speech made it clear that Heydrich was already directing a break from the forced exodus of Jews from Nazi-controlled Europe. "Forced labor" is the term for Jews who are sent to East Asia to perform "final solutions", where "doubtless an inordinate amount" of deaths occur from natural causes. Any rest, prior which undoubtedly is one of the most resistance-able parts, must always be treated accordingly. It is a natural option and, if released, could become the nucleus to a new Jewish construction. Most people were familiar with this phrase and the associated terms, such as "displacement", Final Solution," "special therapy" or "evacuation." It was at this time that the East was rampant in the murder of Jews. Despite all the euphemisms being used, this was the intention of the physical destruction of the Jews. The Heydrich plan should have an impact on 11 million European Jews (including British and Irish).

One of those practical measures discussed was to establish a retirement camp in Protectorate Bohemia or Moravia. This will enable it to avoid any intervention in favor of specific Jews. This was the Terezin-ghetto role in 1942.

Wannsee conference, while it did not provide any breakthroughs in the "final" solution nor a decision about the murder of European Jews, was still being conducted. It was first an order to ensure smooth cooperation between imperial office aimed towards "cleansing", or removing, Jews from Europe under the leaderships of Himmler und Heydrich.

23 FEBRUARY, 1942

Near the Turkish coastline, the ship Struma was carrying Jewish refugees bound to Palestine. Only 768 of the victims survived the disaster.

March 9, 1942

Protectorate government directive on preventive combating Gypsy nuisance

10 MARCH 4242

Belzec extermination prison was the first step towards mass murder. Only weeks later, about 30,000 Lublin Jews were murdered by the local gas chambers.

Belzec

The first extermination camp for Polish Jews was established near Belzec in southeast Lublin. It is located near the border of Poland's General Government, which was occupied by Soviet Union. The Germans created the camp initially as a Jewish labor camps. Prisoners were required to build fortifications, anti-tank defenses, and other defensive measures against Russian troops. It was closed at year's end.

A year later, on the 1st of November 1941, this so-called. Operation Reinhard extermination Camp was established. Mass graves should now be made of old anti-tank ditches. Belzec was built by the first residents. They were soon replaced with Jews from neighboring ghettos. Christian Wirth was the commanding officer and SS -Hauptsturmfuhrer Christian Wirth. Wirth already has experience in the euthanasia execution program. German and Ukrainian soldiers were also included in the staff. They had been trained in Trawnikach. Averaging 700 to 1000 Jewish workers, they worked just a few short days before being sent to gas chambers. They were expected to perform the same tasks in Treblinka. These women were required to use the zumzitkovavaly, or gassed, hairs of their wives as materials for making footwear (for military uses).

First three were placed in the camp gas rooms. All doors were fitted to the gas with a rubber gasket. This made the engine of 250 horsepower fit in the shed right next to the house. (A device designed by Commander Ch. Wirth used the Chelmno area for his excursions. The chambers were ready to be used for trial at the beginning of February 1942. Jews from Lubycza Krolewska were then brought to the chambers. On March 17, 1942, was the first transport of Jews out of Lublin.

In the four first weeks, 30,000 Lublin Jews were killed. 15,000 Lviv Jews were killed. 000 Galicia Jews were taken from 35 other ghettos.

The Sobibor and Treblinka procedures were both followed in the preparation for the liquidation and during the actual liquidation. An inscribed sign with the Polish phrase "Attention" stood at the camp's entry. Hang all my items, including money, personal documents, and valuables, here. Shoes Tie a pair of footwear and take it to the designated spot. Don't forget to take your shoes off before you enter the shower.

The extermination at camp was stopped in mid-April 1942. The camp concluded that the gas chambers are not capable of holding enough gas and it must be increased. The old premises were destroyed and a new structure was built. The six chambers measure 5 x 4 meters and can hold 1 000 to 1200 people. It can hold approximately half the number people than the twenty wagons. An "Showers/disinfecting facilities" sign was displayed above the building's entrance.

They began arriving transports in the second half of July. Between July and Oktober 1942, 130,000 Jews came from Krakow, or 225,000 from Lviv. The transports also carried Czech, Austrian, German Jews who had previously been sent to Polish ghettos. It was also planned to bring 200,000 Jews from Romania. However, the Romanian government refused.

Since August 1942, Gottlieb Hising has been the camp commander SSHauptsturmfuhrer Gottlieb. He takes the place of Ch. Wirth was promoted as inspector for the Operation Reinhard extermination camps.

The activities of the camp came to an end at the beginning of December 1942. The vast majority (and only) of Jews in the General Government were released and management decisions were made. Sobibor and Treblinka continued and Auschwitz-Birkenau was closed.

Between December 1942 - the spring of 1943, the mass graves were opened. The victim's body was then burned. The rails grates for the incineration and destruction of corpses were used to accomplish this purpose. The remains of the extermination camp have been destroyed. 600 prisoners who helped during cremation were killed in Sobibor. Two Ukrainian policemen were later moved to the farmhouse located on the site. Belzec, which was occupied by the Red Army of Poland in 1944, was liberated.

Belzec tried to escape some people, but Rudolf Reder is the only one who survived. He managed escape in November 1942. After the war, he wrote a personal testimony on his life in the camp.

In total, 600,000. people were killed at camp Belzec between the 7 months and 7, mostly Jews and a few hundred Roma.

END OF MARITCH 1942

The beginning of mass deportations for Auschwitz.

MARCH 26, 1972

Slovak Jews were first deported. October 20, 1942 was the completion of the first wave.

24 APRIL 1952

Jews were not allowed to use public transport within the empire.

29 APRIL 1972

The Netherlands required that Jews marked the Jewish star.

May 27, 1942

Belgium ordered Jews to mark the Jewish Star.

May 27, 1942

Prague saw the assassination on June 4 of Reinhard Hidrich. He died after sustaining serious injuries.

7 JUNE 1942

France introduced mandatory labeling of Jews Jewish stars in the occupied area.

June 10, 1942

Reinhard Heydrich assassinated, so the village Lidice was exterminated.

11 JUNE 1942

Eichmann's office ordered deportation orders for Jews from Holland. Belgium and the occupied French territories.

July 22, 1942

Put into operation Treblinka extermination camp. 870,000 Jews were killed in August 1943.

July 22, 1942

The Warsaw ghetto was used to begin mass deportations. In September 1942, about 300,000.00 Jews were deported. Most of them lived in Treblinka.

2nd August 1942

Protectorate kept a record of Gypsies, Gypsy halves-breeds as well as the people who live along the gypsy road.

4th September 1942

In Macedonia, the obligatory labeling of Jewish stars has been introduced.

5 OCTOBER, 1942

Heinrich Himmler gave orders to clean up all the Jewish concentration camps in imperial territory.

December 16, 2002

Heinrich Himmler issued a decree deporting Roma to Auschwitz.

17 DECEMBER 1941

Allied declaration condemning Nazi extermination strategy.

1943

26 FEBRUARY, 1943

Auschwitz was the first Romani to be transported. Deportees were sent to a special Gypsy camp.

4-11 February 1943

A number of Jews from Macedonia, Thrace, and Bulgaria were detained by the Bulgarian government. Treblinka saw more than 11,000 people deported.

19 APRIL-16 MAY 1943

Warsaw Ghetto Uprising.

2nd September 1943

Rebellion in Treblinka the extermination Camp

1 - 2 October 1943

German police organizes the event. It aims to deport Danish Jews and arrest them. More than 7,000,000. Most were deported, but they were saved by fleeing Sweden. There were 466 Danish Jews expelled to Theresienstadt.

October 14, 1943

Uprising at Sobibor extermination camps

3 NOVEMBER 1942

The event kicks off Erntefest ("harvest festival"), during which more than 40,000 Jews died in Lublin's camps or ghettos.

1944

March 19, 1944

The German army occupied Hungary.

5 APRIL 1945

Hungary: The Jewish star was worn.

May 15 - July 9, 1944

From Hungary to Auschwitz, 437,000 Jews have been deported.

June 6, 1944

Normandy invasion by the Allies

23 JULY 1945

Visit of the International Committee of the Red Cross (Theresienstadt)

6-7 October 1944

Sonderkommando uprising at Auschwitz. The prisoners managed destroy one of these gas chambers.

1945

17 JANUARY 1946

Commanded Auschwitz to be evacuated. 66,000 prisoners were taken prisoner on a death march.

January 25 -April 25, 1945

50,000 prisoners were expelled on the death marche from Stutthof. 26,000 of these were killed on the march.

January 27, 1945

Auschwitz was liberated with Soviet troops

5 FEBRUARY 1946

Theresienstadt departed 1,200 people in Switzerland.

11th April 1945

Buchenwald was liberated from the US army

29th April 1945

Dachau was liberated and retaken by the US Army.

29 - 30 April 1945

Ravensbruck liberated.

May 2, 1945

International Red Cross detained Terezin

7-8 May 1945

German surrender. The end of Second World War Europe.

18th October 1945

The Nuremberg Trials are beginning.

1947

11 to 29 February 1947

Warsaw hosted the Auschwitz Trial. Rudolf Hoess (ex-commandant Auschwitz) was sentenced and executed during the trial.

NAZI Concentration Camps and Ghettos

From the beginning, the Nazi regime was aggressively challenged with its political opponents and residents given full rights. The Dachau camp was the first koncentrancni facility for political prisoners. The Nazis also created the "Final Solution to the Jewish Question" in 1933, and the camp at Dachau was the first koncentrancni camp for political prisoners. These were neighborhoods that contained separate Jewish communities. Concentration and extermination camps, for their prisoners, were also being built.

www.ingramcontent.com/pod-product-compliance
Lightning Source LLC
Chambersburg PA
CBHW050404120526
44590CB00015B/1815